In this glorious memoir, Diane LeBow weaves together the colorful threads of an adventurous woman's life and takes us along on an invigorating and thoughtful journey through memory, culture, rebellion, and self-discovery.
—**Jasmin Darznik**, New York Times bestselling author of The Bohemians

A celebration of life, love, and travel, Diane LeBow's collection of travel tales, Dancing on the Wine-Dark Sea, is uplifting, inspiring, and full of joy. It's a wonderful read!
—**Linda Watanabe McFerrin**, author of Navigating the Divide, Dead Love, and The Hand of Buddha

LeBow's adventures will amaze you in this smart and funny book.
—**Adair Lara**, former columnist with SF Chronicle, author of Naked, Drunk and Writing: Shed Your Inhibitions and Craft a Compelling Memoir

Coming of age at a time when women were told they should be housewives, Diane LeBow never let anyone tell her what to do. She charted her own course and became a spirited travel writer, opening new worlds to readers. What makes these stories so compelling isn't just the exotic places she visits but the evocative way she describes the people she meets along the way.
—**Michael Shapiro**, author of The Creative Spark and A Sense of Place

Ah, Diane writes from the heart, the same way that she held the cause of Afghan women—and Afghanistan—from the heart! Her writing though paints the scenes of her life so genuinely, true to the soul of each country! Cried and laughed all the way; could not put the book down!
—**Nasrine Gross**, Writer and Activist for Afghan women's rights, President, Kabultec; author, Memories of the First Afghan Girls' High School

Only a woman like Diane LeBow, with her refined sensibility, earthy passion, and consummate love of literature, music, art, horses, cuisine, and politics, could write such engrossing, seductive travel stories; truly a delectable journey of a read, *á la Américaine* abroad.

> —**Camille Cusumano**, author of *The Last Cannoli*; editor Seal Press anthologies, including *France, A Love Story*; staff editor *Via Magazine*

Like Candide seeking "the best of all possible worlds," traveler Diane LeBow seeks the elusive balance between security and adventure. Professor, feminist, activist, horse trainer, backpacker, diver, writer, she cannot be confined by one title, one place—or one love. Her ability to meet and connect with people—in cafes, in rugged mountains, under water, in the air, or bombed-out museums—is astonishing. This lyrical and evocative book will reward the reader who dances with Diane by the wine-dark sea.

> —**Joanna Biggar**, author of *That Paris Year* and *Melanie's Song*

If you've ever been tempted to leave your own circumscribed life and travel to far-flung places like Mongolia, Cuba, or Paris, living as few women would dare, open the pages of Diane LeBow's memoir, *Dancing on the Wine-Dark Sea*. A rollicking romp for the intellectually and culturally curious. A feast of a book.

> —**Adrienne McDonnell,** author of *The Doctor and the Diva*

The author tells of...her self-discoveries in detail, and it's here that the work truly shines... Her learning experiences will be particularly instructive for readers who may have preconceived notions about countries she visited...Overall, the fact that LeBow wrote these stories as she lived through them—and not as an idealized recollection of the past—helps to move the stories along. Vivid description... allows readers to visualize her surroundings.

> —**Kirkus Reviews**

Dancing on the Wine-Dark Sea

Memoir of a trailblazing woman's travels,
adventures, and romance

DIANE LEBOW

GRANITROSE PRESS

Dancing on the Wine Dark Sea
Copyright © 2021 Diane LeBow
All rights reserved. No part of this publication may be reproduced, distributed, or transmitted in any form or by any means, including photocopying, recording, or other electronic or mechanical methods, without the prior written permission of the publisher, except in the case of brief quotations embodied in critical reviews and certain other noncommercial uses permitted by copyright law. For permission requests, contact the author at https://DianeLeBow.com

Cover and book design: Jim Shubin, BookAlchemist.net
Cover photo: Oleg Doroshenko

ISBN: 978-1-7359954-6-5

And now have I put in here, as thou seest, with ship and crew, while sailing over the wine-dark sea to men of strange speech.

—Homer, *The Odyssey*, 1.178

All women together ought to let flowers fall upon the tomb of Aphra Behn, which is, most scandalously but rather appropriately in Westminster Abbey, for it was she—shady and amorous as she was—who earned them the right to speak their minds.

—Virginia Woolf, *A Room of One's Own*

Contents

Preface—Why I Didn't Stay Home   xi

Part I: Leaving Traditions Behind

1. A Gift from Aunt Bea   3
   —*Launch site: Weehawken, New Jersey*
2. The Grand Tour   13
   —*Falling in love in Europe*
3. The Fertile Lands of Ancient Greece   23
   —*Following in the footsteps of ancient goddesses*
4. Free Fall in Central America   31
   —*From Mayan villages to underwater romance*

Part II: New Possibilities

5. The Trout Baron   45
   —*My future as a French "Baronne"?*
6. Saved by Colette: Seduction in St. Tropez   65
   —*"Come see my yacht," he said*
7. Diving Deep and Letting Go in Egypt   73
   —*How I forgot to visit the Sphinx*
8. Crumbs in an Egyptian Bedroom   79
   —*How do YOU warm your biscuits?*
9. An Unexpected New Year's Eve in Luxor   83
   —*Testing Egyptian machismo*

10. Tea on the Nile: Aswan   93
   —*"I am going to throw," and other mistranslations*

Part III: Taking Chances and New Models

11. An Italian Bedtime Story   99
    —*Hot times on an Italian train*
12. At Home with the Water Buffalo Baronessa   109
    —*Mozzarella and ancient goddesses*
13. Song of the Sirens   117
    —*Greek Island escapades with my feisty mom*
14. Corsica: My Dinner with Terrorists   123
    —*Even terrorists reach middle age*
15. A Neolithic Afternoon   131
    —*Speed dating in the Corsican mountains*

Part IV: Insights

16. A Dead Sea Romance   143
    —*Middle Eastern conundrums*
17. Dancing on the Wine-Dark Sea   159
    —*Audrey's final dance*
18. Love on the Line   163
    —*Courtship before cell phones*
19. The Flotsam and Jetsam of Love   171
    —*Re-collections of a single woman*

20. Women in Morocco 177
    —*Up against the wall but laughing together*

    Part V: Many Ways to Be at Home

21. In Colette's Boudoir 191
    —*At Home in a French Chateau*
22. Cuba 199
    —*Machismo and feminism together at last?*
23. Mongolia: Amazons and Horses 211
    —*Way out in Outer Mongolia*
24. Dinner in Dushanbe, Tajikistan 227
    —*Afghan women's resilience and resistance*
25. At Home in Afghanistan 237
    —*Peace is everything*

Reading Group Discussion Questions 250

Publication Notes 252

Awards 254

Acknowledgments 256

About the Author 259

Why I Didn't Stay Home

From my earliest memories, I was a rebel with a cause. What was my "cause"? I didn't exactly know yet but, growing up in the 1950s, I chafed at the restricted roles available to women and girls.

"One day you'll be a wife and mother and a helpmate to your husband" was a common refrain. While studying pre-veterinary medicine at Penn State in 1957, I was the only woman in a class of 500. My advisor, a male veterinarian, called me into his office and said: "We don't want you here. You're just going to get married. You're wasting our time. You're taking the space away from a man." Such experiences were common in those years.

Later, when the poet Adrienne Rich wrote that women in the latter part of the twentieth century "found ourselves in freefall"—after we had "cut the wires" of women's traditional roles—I understood exactly what she meant. That's where women were then, during the second wave of feminism. We had given up the old models for being women but hadn't yet figured out the new ways. We were falling through space with no parachute. And that's where I remained for a few years, hanging in space. With the burgeoning second wave of feminism, I found context and community as women spoke out and wrote about some of our shared issues.

I've been constructing this book all my life, at least in my head. Even at age four, before I really knew how to write, I took blank notebooks and "wrote" in them. Later as I traveled the world—to almost 100 countries from Europe and Mexico to Afghanistan, Mongolia, and beyond—I learned about other lives and cultures, especially women's worlds, and recorded my perceptions in stories.

When I began my explorations, single was considered a very odd number for a woman traveler. There were a very few pioneers who came before us like Freya Stark in the early twentieth century, who often dressed as a man and traveled throughout the Middle East. Changed attitudes today make it no longer unusual for a woman to be exploring the world on her own.

I've met incredible women and men on my journeys: exiled Afghan women in Tajikistan fighting for women's rights, a one-legged Mujahedeen in Afghanistan who celebrates peace, and an Algerian feminist. I've had dinner with Corsican terrorists, slept in the former boudoir of the French writer Colette, had a love affair with a French baron, dived with sharks in the Red Sea, and crossed the Mongolian steppes in the snow on a horse.

My book is not just about solo travel but also sexual independence. I take my readers behind the curtains for intimate peeks at encounters they may be more comfortable experiencing vicariously. Parts of my book continue some traditions. For example, perhaps Geoffrey Chaucer with his bawdy medieval *Canterbury Tales* led the way as the first erotic travel writer. His work was among my favorite readings when I was in graduate school. Erica Jong's 1973 novel *Fear of Flying* was controversial at the time for its joyous portrayal of female sexuality, selling 20 million copies. These pioneers were inspiring models.

Unlike most travel memoirs that look back at the earlier years of an author's life, the majority of my stories were written as I experienced them over the decades. The world of travelers changed as did I.

This book is about a woman who created the life she wanted to live. It is about romance and travel but also offers encouragement for women to take chances and live their lives fully. Out of the conventional fifties in New Jersey and New York City, I launched myself into a life that women were not supposed to even dream of living. It's exciting to review it all and realize how much I've learned from the worlds I've entered, friends I've made around the globe, and experiences I've lived. Whatever age or gender, finding home within ourselves and in the world is what we all yearn for.

That is what my book is about. I hope you enjoy my tales.

—Diane LeBow

PART I
Leaving Traditions Behind

We cut the wires
Find ourselves in freefall.
—Adrienne Rich, poet

A Gift from Aunt Bea

LAUNCH SITE: WEEHAWKEN, NEW JERSEY

My father's eldest sister, Bea, was the matriarch of our family. Large-bosomed Aunt Beatrice, or Aunt Bea, as we called her, wore a corset that felt like a warrior's armor and almost pulverized me, a child of seven or eight years old, when she pulled me close for the requisite hug. Her gray hair was like a helmet, swirled in what seemed a tight and permanent chignon on the back of her head. From it wafted the strangely sweet odor of pomade. Not a hair on her head was out of place—nor was her indisputable command and self-confidence.

Bea owned and ran an international shoe-exporting business that carried her maiden name: Bea Lebow International Shoe Company. This was unusual for a woman in the 1940s and 1950s. Her other siblings, with the exception of my father, who was the town pharmacist, either worked for or were dependent upon Bea. Her husband—balding, silver-haired, red-faced, and large-bellied Charlie Silverman—worked in her Manhattan shoe warehouse as did her brother-in-law, cigar-smoking Uncle Ben. Her two sisters, Ethel and Alice, were her housekeepers. They lived with their husbands in her rambling old house that sat atop the Palisades overlooking Manhattan where her shoe business was located. The youngest brother, Natie, scrawny and bent, stuttered and walked with a limp. He was the black sheep of the family and seemed to be the scapegoat for everyone's frustrations. Natie was in charge of scrubbing the pots after meals. He lived in a tiny room on the top floor of Bea's house. Other family members yelled at him. Rumored to be a disabled veteran, he seemed to just hang out with locals in town and didn't "go to business," Bea's New York equivalent of "going to work."

When not in New York managing her shoe company, Aunt Bea and Uncle Charlie sailed the world on Holland America Line ships. They traveled primarily for business, but their adventures included a great deal of pleasure. Whenever I visited Aunt Bea's bedroom—she and Charlie each had their own bedrooms—as she was packing for their next voyage, I peeked into the open trunks, which revealed neatly hung rows of colorful sequined gowns as well as phalanxes of shoes in multicolored hues and styles. "For the captain's dinners," Bea explained, leaving it to my imagination to picture these sumptuous events.

"Caracas." "Karachi." "Scheveningen." These place names tripped off the tongue of Aunt Bea. When she and my uncle returned home from their journeys around the world, the scents and stories she bestowed upon us intrigued me and stirred my dreams of adventure and travel. Bea's business included visiting developing countries like Pakistan and Venezuela, North African countries, and European ports. With each homecoming, out of her large trunks came treasures like camel saddles, snakeskin belts, carvings on fossilized woolly mammoth tusks, and bitter-smelling leather purses. "It's only from the camel urine they use in the dyeing process in North Africa. The smell will wear off after a while," Aunt Bea said.

Some of my earliest memories include putting on a dress and patent leather shoes, not easy for a tomboy like me, and attending bon voyage parties in their suite on the huge ship. Adorned with flowers from well-wishers, the parties featured platters of hors d'oeuvres, elegant cakes, and always a well-stocked bar—although no one in the family seemed to drink except Uncle Charlie, whose joviality rose in proportion to his cocktail intake. As a young girl, I wandered the maze of decks, ballrooms, banquet rooms, swimming pools, and corridors that offered glimpses into strangers' staterooms, every corner buzzing with the excitement of imminent departure to new adventures and destinations. Finally, loud ship whistles blew. "All ashore who's going ashore."

I fantasized about trying to stow away. Instead, my parents, older brother Howard, and I exited down the gangplank with the hundreds of other temporary visitors. Standing on the darkened dock in Hoboken, New Jersey, I waved as we tried to spot Aunt Bea and Uncle Charlie high above us on one of the glittering decks. The ship's horns would blast, and slowly the SS *Nieuw Amsterdam* or *Rotterdam* sailed out past the Statue of Liberty and off to ports I had yet to even dream about.

Aunt Bea and Uncle Charlie were storytellers. When they returned from a trip, our large extended family and friends would gather and hear tales of their latest adventures. "And when Charlie"—Bea pronounced his name "Chaarrlee"—"pulled his sheet back in our hotel room in Marrakesh, there on the pillow along with a flower and chocolate was a live scorpion. They told us it was good luck."

Her storytelling was always entertaining—and sometimes a bit naughty. "In Paris, we were invited to a dinner party in a restaurant just off the Champs-Élysées, a very elegant place with waiters in dinner jackets, white tablecloths, crystal, and fine wines. What a surprise that each course came in the shape of some s-e-x activity or private part of the anatomy." Bea somehow always combined a bit of the risqué with traces of Victorian propriety, all seasoned with a coquettish twinkle in her eyes.

Although of Jewish heritage and tradition, my parents were primarily secular. Aunt Bea and her other siblings strictly practiced the Jewish traditions. Every spring my parents, Howard, and I attended the Seder, part of the ritual of Passover, at Aunt Bea and Uncle Charlie's large home. We always regarded the expected chaos of the occasion with amusement. Aunts Ethel and Alice scuttled around the kitchen, basting, sautéing, pulling roasts and rolls out of the oven, mixing bowls awhirl, intermittently shouting, "Where is Natie? Take out the garbage. Run to the store for two more jars of pickled herring, two more packages of matzah, some more tzimmes."

The various rituals and foods of the entire event were mysterious to a child. Uncle Charlie, as the oldest male, presided over the reading of the ritual text, leading multiple required toasts with the sweet Manischewitz wine, produced in New York State, which lubricated the long dinner, although I only touched it to my lips and countered the strong flavor with rolls, turkey, and matzah.

For me, at age eight, there were some highlights, such as when we took turns reading aloud about our ancestors' migration out of Egypt to escape the Pharaoh's oppression and slavery. I would picture their experiences, complete with locust swarms, camel caravans, and sandstorms. Years later, I recalled these tales as I encountered them as a curious visitor to those same lands—even locust swarms when I rode a camel across the North African desert in Libya.

My family often spoke of my grandparents, who left Eastern Europe in the late-nineteenth century during the Jewish pogroms, landing on Ellis Island and settling in Manhattan. I never knew them but was curious about what their lives and voyages were like. What courage to leave everything behind and sail into an unknown new land. Perhaps even as a child, my experience and imagination were whirling me toward a life of exploration and adventure.

At that childhood time, though, there were two special features of these Aunt Bea/Uncle Charlie extended family Seder dinners that I enjoyed. Each year at certain points during the meal and Uncle Charlie's reading of the historical text in Hebrew, everyone would burst into a loud and cheerful song, also in Hebrew. Most of us—certainly me—had no idea what it meant. But the refrain after every stanza was "*dayenu*," which sounded like my name. I was certain that the song was about me and beamed as everyone sang it. Years later, I read a translation of the over-2,500-year-old text and learned that *dayenu* meant "It would have been sufficient," which was part of thanking God for his generosity during the Exodus story.

The other highlight of the Seder was the hiding of the piece of sacred matzah or unleavened bread. The tradition is that the eldest male blesses this piece of matzah, wraps it in a linen napkin, and puts it aside. During various machinations, the youngest child, aided by other adults, steals the *afikoman*, as it is called, and hides it. Later in the reading, Uncle Charlie would look for the blessed piece of matzah and make a big fuss about trying to find it. He needed it to continue the dinner ceremony. Finally, in desperation, he would ask if anyone had seen it. One or more adults would say, "No, but maybe Diane can help." Then Aunt Bea would urge me to ask him how much he would give me to find it. "That child has a *yiddishe kopf*, a Jewish mind," she'd say. Aunt Bea always praised my intelligence, practicality, and independence, emphasizing that I took after her. After a strict bargaining ritual, I would go into another room, returning with the matzah. Uncle Charlie would distribute pieces to everyone at the table, which they would eat accompanied by special herbs and a prayer. One particular year when I was about six years old, I was determined to be really clever at my task, so I spent time in an adjoining room, making some noises with books and furniture, pretending to be hiding it carefully. Later, as they were chewing, Charlie said, "Little Diane, where did you hide the *afikoman* so well?"

Proudly looking around at everyone, I replied, "In my panty."

Bea was good friends with the directors of the Holland America Line and had many contacts in the Netherlands. Some years later in 1961, when I was about to graduate from college and wanted to travel to Europe before beginning my graduate work at the University of California Berkeley, I began to plan a backpack trip there with the man I was dating at the time. He was several years older than me, had graduated, and had a job. His idea was to go over on a tramp steamer or freighter and then take trains, hitchhike, and generally figure it out as we went along. Students backpacking around Europe was a concept that wouldn't take hold for at least five more years.

Although my parents generally gave me the freedom to make my own decisions and were enthusiastic about my travel to Europe, they had some qualms about this casual approach. We were all greatly relieved when Aunt Bea came up with an alternative plan. *Het Nederlandse Bureau voor Buitenlandse Studenten*, the Dutch Bureau for Foreign Students, was offering a six-week Grand Tour of Europe guided by Dutch university students. There would be five American college girls to a VW bus, driven and escorted by a Dutch student. All this for $1,500, an economical price even back then. We would drive through Holland, France, Germany, Italy, Switzerland, Belgium, even Luxembourg and tiny Liechtenstein, all the while experiencing Europe from a European student's perspective. Aunt Bea made all the arrangements for me. My primary interest was going to Europe, and I hadn't been all that comfortable with my boyfriend's "roughing it" plans. Plus our relationship was really more buddies than a big love affair. So I said goodbye to him and started packing.

We set sail on a Holland America Line student ship, which meant we bunked five girls to a cabin with no-frills meals and accommodations. It was comfortable enough and a jolly way to begin my first international adventure. Having just graduated with an English degree, my head was full of stories and characters of American expat writers and their books, including Hemingway and his *The Sun Also Rises* and *A Moveable Feast*. One of my heroes was Lady Brett Ashley, whose short hairstyle, black turtleneck sweaters, and independent style I emulated. During our crossing, the bulletin that came in announcing that Ernest Hemingway had committed suicide touched me personally.

July 2, 1961: Ernest Hemingway, dead of gunshot wound to the head. Ketchum, Idaho.

I felt that I was part of his legacy as I began my travels in Europe.

At the dock in Rotterdam, a young Dutch medical student greeted me and the four other young women I was to travel with. "Hello, I'm Kees."

He was tall, slim, and handsome. All of us—five American recent college graduates and one fairly shy Dutch medical school graduate—piled into a Volkswagen bus. Off we went on our six-week Grand Tour of Europe. Many adventures followed, and my competitive nature won Kees's attention over the four other women in our group. By the end of the six weeks, he and I imagined we were in love.

Kees would be the man I would marry two years later, after completing my graduate work at Berkeley. There in Holland, my travels began in earnest, and they haven't stopped since. I'm sure that Aunt Bea would approve.

The Grand Tour

Falling in Love in Europe

Paris at dusk—or *l'heure bleu*, the "blue hour," as the French say—enveloped me as I stepped out of our Volkswagen bus onto *l'avenue des Champs-Élysées* for the first time. There it was, as I had imagined—the grandeur, lights, traffic, chic store windows, and French chatter all around. Having just completed my degree in English, I was on a Grand Tour of Europe. My brain swarmed with images from Henry James's and Ernest Hemingway's novels about Americans in Europe as well as the poetry of John Keats, Lord Byron, and William Wordsworth. Women writers and poets were rarely part of the literary canon at that time. Aunt Bea, my father's sister, an international shoe exporter and traveler, had arranged the trip for me, an option my family preferred to my plans of backpacking around Europe with my "older" boyfriend. That vagabonding style, though increasingly popular at the time, seemed a bit dicey, even to me, but quite in keeping with my main goal, which was to immerse myself in Europe before starting graduate school at Berkeley in the fall.

Sailing from New York City to Rotterdam on a Holland America Line student ship, five of us to a cabin, was the lively start to our six-week adventure. Upon arrival at the dock, we fifteen newly graduated American college girls, with our virginal suitcases and very likely bodies as well, were met by our guides and drivers: three Dutch recent medical school graduates—Edouard, Jaap, and Kees. We piled into waiting VW buses, five of us to a vehicle. Our itinerary included nine countries during the ensuing six weeks—the Netherlands, Belgium, Luxembourg, Liechtenstein, Germany, Switzerland, France, Italy, and Monaco. Traveling with European students turned out to be an ideal introduction to European life and culture. The Dutch, with their good sense as well as planning and language skills, made superb tourist guides even if they were sometimes a bit stodgy and overprotective. For example, when one of our buses had a flat tire on an Italian road, our Dutch guides, distrusting the southern European Italians, had us stand in a protective circle around the parked buses to ward off possible thieves.

Of the various Dutch expressions I learned, one of my favorites encapsulates the Dutch character so well: "*Dat is onzin*—That is nonsense," referring to anything less than sensible.

There were some hilarious, or *onzin* experiences during our travels. On one of our earliest days together, upon checking into our hotel in a French town as we all discussed plans and the time to meet for dinner, we were shocked when our gentlemanly Dutch escorts asked us, "Would you girls like to have a douche before dinner?"

We all gasped and stared at each other, wondering how to respond. Finally, those of us with some French language skills realized the confusion. Our escorts, like most Europeans, understood "douche "to simply mean "shower," whereas to unsophisticated American girls, especially coming out of the sexually repressed 1950s, the word conjured up something else entirely.

Sometimes, our madcap adventures took odd forms in the middle of the night. After leaving Paris, we drove south into the picturesque French château region. We toured several châteaux and were awed by the soaring towers, sculptures, manicured gardens, fountains, and of course, incredible food. At the end of our first day in the Loire region, our group checked in for our scheduled overnight at a medieval château on a lake near the town of Tours. At dinner, we met several male German university students who were apparently the only other guests in the château. Tired after a long day, my group all retired for the night—two girls to each enormous room furnished with antiques and large windows overlooking the countryside. My roommate at the time and throughout the trip was a feisty and adventuresome young woman named Kitty. Both from East Coast cities, we shared a similar sense of humor and daring in contrast to the other thirteen, who mainly came from small Midwestern towns and seemed more demure. Kitty and I carefully closed the heavy embroidered, ceiling-high drapes but neglected to check if the door to the hallway locked upon closing. Just as I was drifting off to sleep, screams began to echo throughout the château.

Loud knocks on doors were followed by high-pitched cries that rang up and down the halls. Half asleep, Kitty and I pulled up our covers and asked, "What's going on?" The loud knocks and shrieks continued, then, with a loud creak, the door to our room opened, revealing one of the German students who slowly played a flashlight up and down on his naked body. My roommate Kitty and I were startled but more curious than frightened. What was this about? My high school German was sufficient for me to tell the naked male body to get lost. The door slammed behind him as he left, and we had a good giggle. We suspected that our fellow lodgers had decided to have fun with the naïve American girls with this prank. The next morning, the German students had left before breakfast so we never got to confront them. Our female travel companions expressed their shock over the whole experience while our Dutch escorts laughed about it.

One beautiful moonlit night in Italy, where we toured Rome and Florence and Venice, found us in a country village at a local outdoor restaurant. For much of this trip, we felt as though we were actors in a magical film. We were young, and we just floated on travelers' clouds from one experience to the next. All the details of itinerary, reservations, and the other responsibilities associated with normal travel were well looked after. On this evening, full of anticipation and youthful energy, we dressed in our summer frocks and met for aperitifs before dinner. We swayed to the romantic strains offered by violins, flute, and accordion as well as a sensual baritone voice. Grapevines twined over our heads, mingling with the sweet smells of freshly cut grass and fragrant flowers in full bloom. When local men invited us to join them on the dance floor, we eagerly accepted. Not knowing much Italian, I flirted and practiced my three years of college French. The handsome lead singer made a small bow and invited me to join him on the dance floor. As we twirled around, his dark hazel eyes and angular olive cheek close to my face, he addressed me with the most unexpected words: *"Voulez vous couchez avec moi?"* "Would you like to go to bed with me?" I had giggled over this naughty phrase in my women's college French classes, and now a flesh-and-blood European actually whispered it in my ear. Unsure whether to giggle or be shocked, I feigned sophistication and muttered a combination of Italian and French: *"Non, grazie. Je suis ici avec mes amis. Pas possible…"* "No, thanks. I'm here with my friends. It's not possible." Later, I wondered if he was teasing me—or was he indeed serious? What if I'd said *Si*?

Over the course of our six-week adventure, we purchased our requisite tourism passport stamps in tiny Liechtenstein, gambled in Monaco, photographed the *Manneken-Pis* (sixteenth-century "Little Pissing Boy") statue in Brussels, glided down Venetian canals in gondolas wearing beribboned straw hats like the gondoliers, and, under down comforters high in the Swiss Alps, drifted to sleep to the tinkle of cowbells. In Paris, we climbed the *Tour Eiffel*, cruised the Seine, and attended the *Folies Bergère*. Each day, new adventures unfolded.

Throughout the trip, we enjoyed flirting with our young Dutch guides. Because I was with the group in Kees's bus, he and I spent a lot of time together. He was adorable: tall, with sandy-colored hair. He seemed very intelligent if a bit shy. Recently graduated from medical school at Leiden, one of Europe's oldest and most prestigious universities, along with the other two guides, he was about to enter his medical internship and looked forward to a successful future.

Without giving it much thought but, as always, rallying to any competition and wanting to win, I focused on gaining Kees's favor over the other four girls in my bus. Having grown up in the 1950s, a schizophrenic era for women and girls—especially curious and intellectual ones—we were encouraged to study hard and do well in school. But we also tried to always have a date on Saturday night even—if we had to—when it meant acting a bit stupid to make our date feel superior. Flirtation and competing over boys' attention was a well-trained behavior for many of us.

As each of us settled into a daily routine on the bus, I asserted myself as the permanent resident of the front passenger seat, helping Kees with directions and maps. During our evening strolls after dinner, he and I held hands. Acting out my favorite Hollywood movie scenario of a summer romance in Europe, timidly and then more boldly, I enjoyed our kisses beside the Seine, Rhone, Rhine, Tiber, and finally, the North Sea and Holland.

"When we are back in Holland, I want to introduce you to my parents," Kees said. My unfocused dreams of becoming an American expat in Europe, á la Hemingway, began to look possible.

"I'll be at Berkeley working on my MA for the next two years," I said. "Maybe I can finish in eighteen months."

"My stepfather, a geophysicist, did research at Berkeley and always talks about being there and how wonderful California is. Maybe I can do a summer externship at a San Francisco hospital next year," he replied.

By the end of the six weeks, Kees and I imagined we were in love. When we reached Holland, he took me home to meet his family. While the rest of the group enjoyed a special museum visit, we drove to Kees's family's house in the medieval village of Oegstgeest, near the university town of Leiden. Their beautiful seventeenth-century home, with its façade of ancient redbrick and small black-framed casement windows, was like something out of a Vermeer painting. We entered through the large front door to a house filled with art, antique furniture, a friendly cat and dog, and Kees's hospitable mother, stepfather, and two teenage brothers.

During the lunch of traditional pea soup, salad, and hearty country bread served on hand-painted Delft blue china, Kees made a formal but brief speech in Dutch.

"*Ik hou van haar.* I love her," he said.

His mother burst into tears and, turning to me, said in English, "When your son says such words to you, it is something very special." Both his parents as well as his two younger brothers hugged me. I felt pleased but a bit confused. I wasn't sure where I was going with this, but it was exciting and mostly in the future, so I just relaxed and enjoyed the adventure.

A big discussion ensued, mainly in Dutch, which in upcoming years I would have the opportunity to speak fluently. An idea was hatched with which I agreed. They would help me postpone my return plane ticket. Kees and I would spend ten days traveling around England and Scotland, camping most of the time, a chance for us to get to know each other better. His parents offered to loan us their VW convertible, which Kees would take across the English Channel on the car ferry. Our tour was scheduled to end up in London anyway, so he and I would simply continue to travel after the others left. Together, on a sort of honeymoon, we would tour the English Lake District and Scotland.

Our U.K. trip went very well. We camped in farmers' fields, including one that we thought was empty until we were awakened at dawn. Twenty young black bulls encircled our tiny tent, pawing and snorting at us. We visited Robert Burns's home in Ayr, Hadrian's Wall, and the Lake District. We were excited twenty-two year-olds with our futures before us and lots of plans. I think we were as much in love with the unorthodox possibilities as we were with each other.

I flew back to the States and went off to graduate school at Berkeley. Kees spent the following summer as an extern in a hospital in San Francisco while I finished up my master's degree in record time. I wanted to be a fearless world traveler, but at the same time, I had swallowed enough of the fifties' recipes for a traditional woman's life that there was always the doubt that maybe I wouldn't be okay without a man/partner/husband. With Kees, I felt I could have it both ways. I'd marry a Dutch atheist, move to Europe, travel, and write books. Living in Europe certainly trumped my other apparent options: settling down in New Jersey or becoming a scholarly spinster in academia.

Postscript: I did marry and move to the Netherlands, where I lived for four years and taught at the International School. We enjoyed much travel during those years.

Unfortunately, the love of travel exceeded my love of marriage. The marriage ended eventually, but my travels did not. In fact, they'd really just begun.

The Fertile Lands of Ancient Greece

Following in the Footsteps of Ancient Goddesses

I begin to sing of Demeter, the holy goddess with the beautiful hair. And her daughter, Persephone, too. The one with the delicate ankles, whom Hades seized. She was given away by Zeus, the loud-thunderer, the one who sees far and wide.
—Homeric *Hymn to Demeter* (700 BCE)

On our first morning in Greece, my friend Gloria and I headed to breakfast on the outdoor terrace of the Athens Hilton. Facing my eggs Benedict, all I wanted to do was lie flat on the cool terrace floor. So I did.

Waiters in white coats discreetly stepped around me, perhaps interpreting this action as eccentric American behavior. The Greek fascist regime ruled in full force in 1971, and people tended to mind their own business. Gloria and I attributed my wave of nausea to bad airplane food. We proceeded to plan the rest of our trip: first by bus to visit important sites, then by sea to Mykonos and Crete.

I had just broken up with the man for whom I had left my husband. Perhaps the anxiety of learning to live the single life at age thirty-one was stressing my system. When Gloria, a colleague at the California college where I taught, suggested a trip to Greece, I thought, *What better way to mend a broken heart and move on with life?*

Both of us were steeped in Greek literature and history. But in the fertile lands that spawned the beginnings of Western civilization, our *demokratia*, and stories of randy gods and goddesses, I could not have guessed at the irony of my ongoing queasiness.

Our first stop was the famous amphitheater of Epidaurus, an easy day trip from Athens. We also visited Mycenae from where Agamemnon departed for the Trojan War after he sacrificed his daughter, Iphigenia, so the gods would turn up the winds to fill his sails. His wife, Clytemnestra, was not pleased, took a lover during his ten-year absence, and murdered Agamemnon in the bath after he returned. Breaking up with my husband and now ex-boyfriend seemed much less dramatic from this perspective. Clytemnestra was no weeping lily, and her portrayal bolstered me during the next evenings when we were fortunate to view the entire *Oresteia*, Aeschylus's three-part tragedy at the theater of Epidaurus.

Epidaurus was both a healing center—where Asklepios, son of Apollo, cured the ill from all over Greece—and one of the world's oldest theaters. I hoped a visit there would cure my continuing nausea. Following in the footsteps of millions, we climbed high in the enormous amphitheater that once held ten-thousand spectators and tested its legendary acoustics. Our tour guide, so far below on the stage that she seemed a tiny speck, dropped a drachma, and we heard its distinct ping as it hit the stone floor. Then she tore a Kleenex tissue, and, yes, we could hear that as well. We were sitting in what would have been, no doubt, the poor people's seats. I thought about the challenge of getting acoustics right in contemporary theaters and wondered about the many mysteries we can still learn from the ancient Greeks. Beyond the stage and backdrop (the *skene*), mountains rose and clouds floated in a blue sky. These ancient theaters were built to remind us of the connections between our temporal world, nature, and the spheres of the gods.

    My low-grade sickness continued. I began to almost imagine the worst but put it out of my mind. Here I was in the land of my dreams and years of studies. I wanted to relish every moment. A few days later, we wound our way along country roads in a bus fourteen miles east of Athens to Eleusis, site of the Mysteries, the most famous religious rites of Ancient Greece. They date back to 2,000 BCE and earlier. Believed to have come from Egypt via Crete, the cult of Isis—the Earth goddess—later was worshiped as Demeter and finally the Virgin Mary. The site oozed with the energies of ancient lives and powers. I stumbled up and down timeworn stairs, soaking in the heat and odors of summer vegetation. Poppies dotted the surrounding slopes, and cicadas buzzed in the fecund bushes.

I knew that this area was once the terminus of a biannual procession that began in Athens along what was called the Sacred Way. Anyone could participate as long as he or she was not a barbarian (i.e., someone who was not a native Greek speaker) and had not committed blood crimes. As they walked, people, especially prostitutes, called out dirty words and obscene jokes. All things sexual were celebrated as natural, and fertility was acknowledged as primary to life. The overall celebration marked Demeter's reunion with her daughter, Persephone, when she returned from her six-month annual sojourn with Hades, god of the underworld, who had kidnapped her. During her daughter's months in the underworld, Demeter was too sad to tend to fertility, hence plants and vegetation died and winter set in. As part of these spectacular ceremonies, ancient myths also reported that Persephone was reborn from her mother in the midst of huge fire and brilliant lights seen for miles around. Bulls and phalli were part of these rituals, depicted in frescoes as far away as Minoan Crete and Pompeii. So were fasting and hallucinogenic drink, probably *kykeon*, made with water, barley, and, some believe, the same fungus sometimes associated with the Salem Witch Trials. None was served during our visit!

Here, amidst this ancient place of orgies and bloody sacrifice, the thought that I could be pregnant flashed through my mind. If so, what would I do? I was on my own. I couldn't afford to stop my work, both teaching college and training horses. No one was going to take care of me. I wondered if I would be able to get an early flight home after our visit to Crete. I would deal with the situation later.

After I'd vomited over some of the most fertile sites of Western culture—Delphi, Epidaurus, Mycenae—we decided to save money by taking the ferry over from Piraeus to Crete. What we were not aware of was that the *meltemi,* the hot winds of August, blew heavy on the Aegean. Because of these relentless winds, the ancient Greeks avoided open sea travel as much as possible during this time of year. We soon discovered why. What was typically a nine-hour overnight voyage took almost fifteen hours. I lay on the center of the top deck, watching Orion and the Seven Sisters rock back and forth overhead. After downing seasickness pills, which had little or no effect, I finally read the directions and noticed a bold-print warning: "Do not take during pregnancy as it may cause birth defects to fetus." I began to panic at the thought that I was carrying a deformed fetus.

When we reached the terra firma of Crete, we checked into our economy hotel. Exhausted and hot, I longed for a cool shower and a nap. I stepped into the shower and lathered up with shampoo, sending soap bubbles everywhere. Just as I began to rinse off, the water and electricity shut off simultaneously. "Help!" I shouted to Gloria. "Please bring me the drinking water carafe." I was thinking I could at least wash the shampoo out of my eyes. She brought it in and placed it on the closed toilet-seat cover, failing to notice the lid was rounded. I heard a loud crashing sound. The glass water bottle that offered my last best chance of rinsing my stinging eyes slid off and fell to the Minoan-style tiled floor, surrounding me with what was now a mixture of glass fragments and soap-bubble suds.

"Do I hear the tinkle of tea things?" came the cultured voice of the elegant young Ivy League male student we'd met on the voyage over who was also staying at our hotel. Gloria opened the door to let him in, and there I stood in the semidarkness: draped in a towel surrounded by a moat of foam and glass chips, a far cry from Aphrodite rising from the sea. We all had a relaxing laugh, especially as he was carrying a bottle of retsina.

The next day, we visited the Palace of Knossos, home of the Bronze Age Minoan people and source of the legends of King Minos, Theseus, the Minotaur, and the original Labyrinth. Women had a substantial role in this ancient society, evidenced in frescoes that depicted their participation in bull dancing, in royal dress, and in commanding poses. I especially wanted to marvel at the flush toilet and bathtub that the Minoan queen enjoyed four-thousand years ago. *Probably better than my recent experience at my hotel,* I thought. I wondered what her life was like. Having a daughter to carry on a woman's lineage was central in this matrilineal culture.

However, in my case, any pregnancy was unintended and, in my own life, parenthood was not an option—neither for me nor my former partner.

That evening, Gloria announced she was leaving to tour with a professor from Germany she had met during our ferry crossing. "There's no point in my staying with you," she said. "You're sick and can't do anything. I may as well have fun." Even though she had never been a very caring friend, this news was startling.

I felt abandoned but decided it was time to make some decisions. Changing my Pan Am return ticket home,

I booked a flight from Herakleion to Athens and from there caught my flight back to San Francisco, happily forfeiting my return ferry ticket.

Back in California, life was crazy for a while as my fertility, which percolated during my weeks amongst ancient Greek sites of creativity, caused me to doze off intermittently. This was a challenge as I was teaching college classes each day and training show horses professionally. While I was lecturing about Greek literature, I could hear my own voice fading out and would have to wake myself up. However, it had become increasingly clear that I was, in fact, pregnant. But I didn't want to admit it. It was not something I could handle at the time, so I knew I had to end it. Not an easy decision for most women, but in my case, absolutely necessary. Fortunately, abortions had recently become legal in California.

At a major horse show the week after I'd returned, I was mounting a champion Morgan mare I'd trained for some Bay Area millionaires. After I pulled my foot from the stirrup and returned to the ground to do a brief upchuck, the society lady who'd employed me said, "Could you be pregnant?"

"Oh, no," I replied. "It's that darn Greek food."

Freefall in Central America

FROM MAYAN VILLAGES TO UNDERWATER ROMANCE

I had stayed at the market too long. I was in the mountainous Quiche region of northern Guatemala. It was dusk when I boarded the last bus as it pulled out for a two-hour journey down a winding dirt road to a junction where I hoped to catch a bus back to the small town of Huehuetenango. That was where I was living with a family for a month to learn Spanish and more about their world. The bus was filled with Quiche market women, pigs, chickens, and me. The women, at first, made me feel tense and alone. All were speaking in the Mayan dialect, their skin was dark from the sun, and their wrinkled mouths smiled at me half-toothless. But soon enough, their energy, the smells of their wool weavings, their animals, food, and bodies transported me to another world—theirs. We sat, three on a seat intended for two, surrounded by their chickens and piglets. Using bits of Spanish and lots of body movement, we began to communicate, and they offered to act as my guide and mediator to hand my bus fare to the attendant, a local Quiche man. Soon we were friends exchanging expressions—Quiche for English, using

Spanish as the medium—their Spanish and mine being equally sparse. Like Mary Poppins, I would stick up a finger: "*Uno*, one." Everyone, including the driver, would repeat, "One," then explode into laughter, half from embarrassment, half from pride of accomplishment.

"*Donde usted?*"

"California."

"*Qué tipo de país es ese?*" ("What kind of a country is that?")

They had never heard of California. I realized the otherness of this world to me and then gradually felt more comfortable with them than I had anywhere in a long time. These women made me feel at home among them. I was carrying with me a blanket that I had bought at their mountaintop market. If I wished, I could go home with one of these women and curl up in this blanket at her hearth.

I was traveling alone in a new land for the first time. This had not been the plan. I had embarked on this journey with a female companion. I met Gail at a Berkeley party. She was the director of a major travel company and had lots of information on Guatemala, a place I wanted to visit. I had been reading about recent archaeological excavations in the Mayan area, and as a professor of women's studies and literature, I was very interested in learning more about the roles of women in that civilization. Gail was another single woman with wanderlust. She had time and money. She was bright and seemed pleasant enough. Gail agreed to take care of all the basic arrangements: flights, routing, hotels, and car rental. I said, "Sounds great."

As it turned out, we were dreadful travel companions. She was regimented—an early-to-bed-early-to-riser who measured every step and penny with a calculator. For me, every moment on the road is like a Christmas gift. I like to be surprised. I also make new friends easily, something Gail had trouble understanding. At Tikal, one of the most glorious of the Mayan archaeological sites near the border between Guatemala and what was then British Honduras, now Belize, Peter, a local man in his thirties, asked if he might join us at our table after dinner. It was the 1970s, Tikal excavation was newly underway, and tourism to Mayan sites was in its infancy. We were staying at a small thatched-roof guesthouse, the only visitor facility at the site, and were its only guests. "I work for the various archaeological teams when they are here. I've always lived here, so it is fun for me to show people around," said Peter. Of course, I said yes.

At dinner, a brief rainstorm poured down on the thatched roof. Through the open spaces in the walls that served as windows, the smells of rainforest wafted in. The squawks of wild parrots along with shrieks of the prolific monkey population were our after-dinner music. Even though I had lived in Europe for several years during my early marriage, this was my first peek into worlds far in space, time, and timbre from my own.

When we were back in our room, Gail frowned and said, "Don't you realize if you speak so freely with strange men, they get the wrong idea about you?" The next morning when Peter gave us a private tour of the temples and surrounding jungles, Gail complained of the humidity and mosquitoes.

Several days later, after a lovely drive through the mountains, Gail and I found lodging just outside of the town of Panajachel beside Lake Atitlán at the only hotel at that time, a pink confection of pale-rose stucco walls and white trim with spiral towers that looked out at the volcanic lake. As I sat on the balcony outside our room, I watched the sunset colors play over the lake. Canoes propelled by local Mayan men passed by on the inlaid pink and blue, stroking like swallows into the sun path, all the way home to a tiny village in a crease of a volcano beside the watery kaleidoscope that stretched before me. The colors dropped and flowed from spot to spot, now clear-cut shading, now ruffled ornate clouds.

That's when Gail asked from inside the room, busy at her pocket calculator: "Do you remember what we tipped the taxi driver in Guatemala City? And how much did we spend on stamps in the post office in Antigua?" At that moment, I realized that to be there with myself and the sounds, smells, and sights of this lovely land along with the local people was what I wanted. That I was unafraid of being alone or of loneliness. The next day, I parted company with Gail. Like a guilt-ridden divorcee, I was willing to offer any sacrifice to remove myself from her, even giving up our rented car to her in the middle of the mountains of Guatemala.

If I hadn't said goodbye and hitched a ride farther into the mountains, I never would have met the Quiche market women. Nor would I have heard of the magical isle of Roatán off the coast of Honduras.

"Tegucigalpa." I liked pronouncing the name of the capital of Honduras.

After a couple of weeks in the northern mountains of Guatemala, I had started dreaming of tropical isles. Swimming in a warm clear sea over the holidays sounded lovely. In a few days, it would be Christmas. In the market in the colorful and historic market town of Chichicastenango, I met a young American anthropologist who was studying the many words in Mayan dialects for the color green. "Check out Roatán," he said in answer to my tropical island query.

"To get to Roatán, you must first take a bus back to Guatemala City. Then you get a plane to Tegucigalpa. From there, twice a week—sometimes once, you never know—you get a one-hour flight to La Ceiba. That is on the east coast of Honduras. You can ask there when the next flight over to Roatán will be."

Our small propeller plane landed in the rain on an oozy muddy runway. A broken sign read "Roatán Airport." We'd sat three across in seats suitable for two on the forty-five-minute flight over; I was sandwiched between two Baptist missionaries because the plane was overbooked as it usually was. There seemed to be no schedule, and no one could say when the next plane would fly over to Roatán from La Ceiba—a dreary, broken-down-shacks, unemployed-men-outside-the-bars kind of town that I was not eager to explore in great detail. The missionaries must have sensed an opportunity for a healing act when they saw the desperation on my face. They were already safely stuffed into the dilapidated stomach of the La Ceiba Airlines plane.

"Full; no room," said a skinny young man in a dirty peaked cap that had been an official's hat for someone at some point. The missionaries seemed to have a regular hold on the flights to and fro. One of them signaled at me through the doorway to come on in. Maybe they sensed a potential convert. I was in. The skinny young man twisted a couple of wire hangers around the broken hinges of the airplane door with the help of two missionaries to hold it more or less in place, and we took off.

The week before, a travel agent in Guatemala had given me the name of a hotel, the less expensive one of two on Roatán. Its name, Spyglass Hill, sounded sufficiently nautical and efficient. When he booked the hotel, I hadn't thought about it being the rainy season. Warm sheets of rain soaked me and my gear as I stood on the muddy airstrip, trying to keep the icy mud from sucking my sandals off my feet. "Spyglass Hill?" I asked a man unloading baggage from the plane. He pointed toward a lopsided van at the edge of the strip. I sucked my feet over in that direction. "Spyglass Hill"? I repeated to a fellow with sunken cheeks and a brown cigarette hanging from his lips. He was standing near the van, possibly the driver. He jerked a thumb toward the open back door, took my pack, and tossed it on top with a crate of chickens and various burlap sacks and wet cardboard boxes. Inside the musty interior, various people, small like me, pushed closer together to allow me to place a part of my rear on a torn and wobbly seat.

For two hours, we drove through rainforest along flooded dirt paths, dropping off this passenger and that one at tiny hamlets, individual shacks, or just beside trees that apparently were near someone's home. Finally, I was the only passenger. I started to worry. In my limited Spanish, I asked if we were still heading toward Spyglass Hill. The driver said something that sounded like "umm-huh," swept his hand toward the dirty windshield, and pointed through sheets of rain as there were no windshield wipers.

Through the pouring rain, I could see a bit of the Caribbean. "Spyglass Hill," the driver said while jerking his thumb toward a white building. I stepped out, reflecting that *this* was my first Caribbean experience. Advertising for Caribbean getaways flashed in my mind. Bronzed couples laughing as they ran along a pristine beach. "Soak in the sun." "You deserve some pampering."

Instead, a scrawny man, eyeglasses dripping with rainwater, ran toward me. He grabbed my pack and motioned me to follow him.

"I'm Bill," he said in an American accent. Fumes of alcohol billowed from his mouth, but he seemed very hospitable. "My wife, Katy, is in the kitchen working on dinner. How was your trip?" I had a sinking feeling about being stranded. Why had I chosen to come to this isolated place? Poor me. Christmas Eve, and I was all alone. When was the next plane out?

Bill showed me to my room. Exhaustion settled

over me. I limped to the window and looked out. Sweet smells of guava and warm sea air filled my nostrils. Two large macaws croaked a greeting from a vine just off my balcony. Aside from the sounds of the jungle and the sea coming in over the reef were silence and peace, and just down the slope from the hotel, over the tangle of trees and vines, the dark-turquoise Caribbean. I changed out of my wet clothes and went down to dinner.

The next morning, I sat by the pool in the brilliant sunshine watching the dive instructor teach a Colombian couple and their son—the only other guests at the hotel besides me—the preliminaries of scuba diving. "Want to join us? I'll get you ready to dive with us this afternoon," the instructor offered.

"No, I'm just watching. It's too dangerous for me."

The instructor's name was Jarka. Originally from Czechoslovakia, he had been a ski guide in Colorado until he transformed himself into a scuba instructor. A man in his late thirties sporting an athletic compact body topped by a round face and blue eyes, Jarka told me he wrote fiction and sketched. I was entranced and decided to give diving a try.

On my first dive, he held my hand as I became accustomed to this world of weightlessness and diffused beams of light from a surface sixty to one-hundred feet above my head. Scuba diving is meditation. Gravity gone, I learned to do backflips and stand on my head—which I have never been able to do on dry land. The only sounds were my inhalations and exhalations. The Caribbean Sea is warm and comforting, usually almost as calm as a pool, with clear visibility sometimes descending one-hundred feet or more. We swam amidst hundreds of silver tarpons and soared with manta rays, dinner-plate-sized queen angelfish, silver barracudas, blue-and-gold parrotfish with beaklike mouths that bite off coral. Most people don't realize those white sandy beaches are really parrotfish shit. Soft gorgonian corals danced around us. Jarka showed me how I could climb inside the giant barrel sponges that reminded me of large burnt-sienna-colored Roman vases.

In addition to the underwater world, he helped me explore Roatán. At first, I was only aware of the many magical qualities of the island: the soft warm breezes, the sunsets, the sounds of sea and birds, the scent of rainforest, the tastes of fresh fish, mango, and guava. I had to learn that walking on the beach at dusk marked me as dinner for thousands of no-see-'ems, those tiny insects that are ninety-nine-percent mouth. Subsequently, I had the opportunity to view one through a microscope, and it was a frightening experience. By the end of my stroll, on my second evening on Roatán, I had more than five-hundred no-see-'em bites all over my legs that swelled into itchy welts. Jarka brought me plastic buckets filled with ice water in which I soaked an itch that no scratching could ease. There was another itch that Jarka helped me out with as well. After we went horseback riding was when I realized Roatán horses carry ticks. Jarka suggested he check me for wayward ticks. Sure enough, they had traveled way off normal tick country. Searching for any leftover ticks became a nightly ritual, and soon we forgot about the ticks.

I stayed at Spyglass Hill for two weeks longer than I had planned. During that time, the proprietor, Bill, spent much of his time typing away on mystery novels, sipping rum over ice, and talking to strangers on his ship-to-shore radio. "I'd love to stay longer," I told him, "but I'm expected back in San Francisco next week." There were no phones on the island.

"No problem. Just give me the name and number of a friend you want me to contact. I'll talk with another ham radio operator stateside and ask them to call your friend and tell them you are delayed. We do this all the time." The next day, Bill assured me he'd made contact with a man in Texas who promised to call my friend David in Berkeley. I had just started dating David a couple of weeks before I left, and he was planning to pick me up at San Francisco Airport on my scheduled return. As it turned out, he never got the message I was coming back two weeks later, so he went to the airport repeatedly to meet flights coming in from Guatemala City. He reported me to the U.S. Bureau of Missing Persons. They began a search for me. When I did return, David was understandably furious, and I was in love—with the adventure of travel, with islands, with diving, and with Jarka Dvorak.

Three of these loves stayed with me for life. Three out of four—not bad.

Back in Santa Cruz, I received a letter from Jarka. He had eloped with the wife of the American cultural attaché to Honduras who had arrived at Spyglass Hill the day I was leaving. I told this to Tillie Shaw, a poet and women's studies professor at the University of

California Santa Cruz, where I was working on my doctorate on the History of Consciousness, focusing on cross-cultural feminist history, while teaching classes. At that time, the irony of the interstices between my chosen specialty and my life had not yet dawned on me. Tillie's response to my heartache: "I'm so glad to be finished with all that."

But I still had many miles to go before I would be able to understand what she meant.

PART II
New Possibilities

Hearts may be broken, men may come and go,
but the cows must be milked.
—Ellen Glasgow, novelist

The Trout Baron

My Future as a French *Baronne*?

I found Paris especially difficult to leave that morning. Familiar buildings and monuments glistened with fresh snow that had fallen during the night. Teary-eyed, I almost fell as I skidded over the medieval cobblestones of my Marais apartment courtyard for the last time. The cabby studied me in his rearview mirror.

"Why are you leaving Paris?"

"Because I must return to my job and home in San Francisco."

"Tsk-tsk"—the ultimate French negation—and a slow-motion shake of his head registered the cab driver's displeasure.

"What matters in life is that you make love with someone you care about on Sunday morning and walk out with them on Sunday afternoon," he counseled me. "It's not good to live your life alone."

After my two years in France, I had an enviable apartment, interesting friends, even the offer of a professorship in Paris teaching women's studies. The various strands of my life were finally weaving together. Why leave now? That old recurrent battle percolated once again inside me: love and security versus freedom and adventure.

The cabby's words touched a sensitive spot. The second wave of feminism which began in the late 1960's prompted many of us to give up the old ways of being women, but we hadn't quite figured out the new guidelines. It was like floating through space without a ripcord to pull. Sometimes, it was lonely out there. Occasionally, I felt like coming in for a landing.

At the airport, in the crush of the crowded waiting room, I nudged my possessions toward the check-in counter: two oversized suitcases, three boxes, and a portable computer. I felt like a contemporary version of Hannibal crossing the Alps—minus the elephants.

"*Madame, s'il vous plaît?* May I help you?" A dignified man in a tweed jacket appeared beside me. For a moment, I expected a Maurice Chevalier refrain to spring from his mustachioed lips. His kindly face was lined but robust, sophisticated, and attractively sensual; his salt-and-pepper hair, well-cut wool clothing, and perfectly shined mahogany cordovan shoes announced substance and dependability. Like a hero from a fairy tale, he exuded an otherworldly serenity.

We chatted our way up to the counter. "*Je m'appele Serge de Kervoisin?* Shall I see if I can arrange our seats together?" Somewhere over the mid-Atlantic, it became clear this could be the start of something. He was a baron from northern Brittany, tracing his ancestry back to the Romans. He had two chateaux left, was land-rich and cash-poor, and raised what cash he needed by selling off lumber from his forests and raising trout. I felt as if we were acting out a Henry James novel: I, the young—well, not that young, naïve, but energetic New Worlder; he, the highly cultivated, somewhat jaded and fading European.

The narrow seats encouraged our shoulders to touch. When he poured my wine and toasted to our serendipitous meeting, the sides of our hands brushed ever so slightly. I had never known a man like Serge; in his early sixties, he was sixteen years older than I.

By the time the flight reached our destination, I had offered to delay my departure for San Francisco for a few days to help him explore New York for the first time. He had the use of a friend's vacant apartment on the Upper West Side of Manhattan, and I stayed with old friends.

"One of the reasons I've come to the States is to establish connections with antique dealers," he said. At the Metropolitan Museum of Art, Serge taught me about the nuances of the furniture collections, which helped me to look at small curves and carvings with a new awareness. I tried to concentrate on the collections, but more absorbing was how the lines of his jaw and cheeks changed from shadow into light when he spoke. How amusingly his elegant dignity contrasted with his brightening demeanor when I touched his hand or said, "What fun you are to be with," or "I've never known a man like you."

Just around the corner from the furniture collections was one of my favorite rooms in the museum. "Come look at the Temple of Dendur. This was a goddess temple.

Did you know that in pre-Christian times, to make love with a temple priestess was considered a sacrament?" He opened his eyes wide at this bit of information.

"Well, well. Now it's time for some tea, don't you think?"

Our week together passed swiftly: towering corned beef on rye at the Carnegie Deli; a Broadway musical, *42nd Street;* elegant and romantic small restaurants; a boat trip from the Hudson to the East River; more museums; and finally, slow and precise lovemaking in his temporary apartment. I had never made love with a man so much older than me, nor one of Serge's background. He too seemed a bit nervous the first night I went home with him.

"Let's have a drink. I quite like your American bourbon." He quickly downed one glassful and poured another. He embraced me gently, kissing me in a preliminary way as though he were testing the waters, then more firmly, opening my lips with his tongue. His immaculate manners extended into his lovemaking. Slipping off his clothes quickly, he slid under the sheets. As I undressed, he pointedly looked away, and then welcomed me to join him under the covers. In my travels, I have found that lovemaking techniques vary according to culture, class, and age of participants. This was my first time with a French aristocrat, and I was not disappointed.

The following month, when I was back in San Francisco, along with the first signs of spring, letters and cards began to arrive on both sides of the Atlantic. Our writing, like our conversations, moved back and forth between French and English, which was perhaps emblematic of our striving to bridge emotional and cultural ravines.

"*Belle Dame*, I don't forget you," he had written shortly after our January meeting. "I keep a very pleasant memory of our romantic encounter, and I would like to renew it. Love and kisses, Serge de Kervoisin."

Finally, in May, I found myself writing: "*Cher Serge, Merci* for your wonderful letter and the sprig of lavender. It still has a beautiful scent and makes me think of spring in the French countryside. . . . In just 30 days, I will be back in Paris and look forward to accepting your invitation to visit you in Bretagne. I shall let you know when I have a clearer view of dates and so on.... *Je t'embrasse.*"

And so, after a few months of exchanging letters, the summer found me in Brittany at the Manoir de Kervoisin. Serge met me in Paris and we drove out to his manor. Tall rows of plane trees formed bowers over our heads as we entered the long driveway. On the right stood a small, abandoned, but perfect half-timbered château dating from the fifteenth century; Queen Anne once stayed there. Opposite it stood the fairy-tale cottage in which he lived; this had been converted from an ancient watermill. Behind the cottage were laid out more than seventy enormous tanks in which trout were bred and raised. All around the cottage and into the distance were well-tended shrubs, flowers, and vegetable gardens. The sound of running water from the tanks permeated the air, as did some slight odor of fishiness when I stood amid the pools.

"During the winter of the great floods twenty years ago, all the trout escaped," Serge recalled. I looked at the open-air tanks teeming with swarming trout, the dense population arranged according to size and age. Never again would I bite into a fresh pan-fried trout served with small white parsleyed potatoes without remembering those trout swimming in the shit of a thousand other trout.

I thought about the fish suddenly liberated from their suffocating confinement during those floods. What a surprise for a trout to be suddenly swimming in flood tides with much of western Brittany as its sea. Did they long for the safety and surety of their tank? Or did they relish chance encounters and freedom—until the floods receded and they found themselves stranded, out of their element?

"*Monsieur le Baron!*" My short course in *pisciculture* was interrupted by a medieval-looking farmhand wearing a large yellow rubber apron, baggy overalls, and brown rubber boots that came up just above his knees. The worker's ruddy, carbuncled face reflected many years in the rains and winds of Brittany. With his pale-blue eyes, muscular forearms, and thumb in a dirty bandage, he could have just slipped out of a Breughel painting.

Serge gave instructions to his servant concerning the feeding of the fish, removal of equipment, and preparation for tree cutting. Serge's limberness and vitality belied his sixty-four years. He talked about how his ancestry dated back to Roman times via Flanders, and his two châteaux had been in his family since the fourteenth century—but that titles and land did not necessarily translate into cash. Unfortunately, because they were more than five hours' drive from Paris, the châteaux and trout farm were almost unmarketable. So, with his modest stands of oaks, his trout-breeding operation, and his vegetable garden, Serge lived a life out of time and almost totally self-sufficient.

The warm sun soothed my travel-weary shoulders, and drowsiness seeped through me. I felt more content within myself than I had in a long time, safe and cared for.

"*Venez. Venez. S'il vous plaît.* Come in, please, I want to show you my mill house, my cottage." Serge used the ancient Breton word *penti* for cottage and always addressed me with the formal "*vous.*" It was part of his traditional old French ways. When I mentioned it, he explained it reflected the respect and esteem he felt for me. At first, such formality seemed odd, but as I became accustomed to it, I too felt myself playing into an appropriate role: no longer a visitor from California but a special woman, selected by chance to be playing a part in this tale.

The water-mill cottage was painted a pale salmon with gray stone corners and dark timber trim. It was covered with vines and pink and red climbing roses. Crossing the curved bridge to the front door, the air, scented with the sweetness of roses and herbs, caressed my cheeks. The inside of the cottage had the feel of a place that had been lived in and well-tended for centuries. In the large stone fireplace, a fire crackled, illuminating Serge's guitar, easel, writing desk, and book-lined shelves.

The typical French country kitchen contained an old stove, a gray stone sink, and fresh green vegetables gathered in a basket. A row of windows overlooked a small orchard of fruit trees and flowers. I felt as if I had come home to Grandmother's house—but instead of Grandma, here was this lovely man who might have just walked off the screen of a Hollywood version of a French romance.

Later, Serge removed an antiquated grilling rack from the wall beside the living-room fireplace and used it to cook our steaks over the fire. He sang and played old tunes for me on his guitar, including Jacques Prévert's *"Il y a longtemps que je t'aime. Jamais je t'oublierai."* ("I have loved you for a long time. I shall never forget you.") This song always touched me with its poignant mix of sadness yet hopefulness concerning the possibility of love. Over our cognacs, he asked, "Have you ever thought you might marry again?"

I paused. Probably that Parisian cab driver was right. Love, continuing and unconditional: This is what mattered in life. On the other hand, marriage had long seemed to me a trap, and I usually spoke against it. Somehow, here in this peaceful atmosphere with this kind and interesting man, it didn't seem such an impossibility. What would it be like to be a *baronne*? I could actually follow my dream and move to France—but in a very different way than I had envisioned.

"Maybe. I don't know. I haven't thought about it," I said.

Certainly, Serge seemed healthy and stable as well as generous and considerate. Even lovemaking had a flair; it was almost like being at a fancy dress ball or tea party but also a feeling of home. It was passion without lust, intimacy without sentimentality, total pleasure without concern for past or future. It was like the best of conversations with the closest, most interesting of your friends. One morning as we embraced in his large bed, pushing aside the bolsters, I complained that the long, narrow, cylindrical cushions gave me a stiff neck. He joked: "French pillows haven't changed since the eighteenth century. But I'll find you another pillow. Let me show you something though; these bolsters work quite well in certain positions." Proceeding to demonstrate, he pushed one under my hips.

Someone once joked that little French boys are taught to be good lovers right along with their history and grammar lessons. Our orgasms came and went with pleasure but without the disruption of a larger flow of communication. Serge explored my body with care, tenderness, and genuine interest—like he was visiting a new country. His body was taut and fit; the maturity of it excited me. How much of life it had experienced, like the collected memories inside his chateau. Making love with Serge was like being in that ancient space. Confinement with a great view. I called him *mon petit chou*, my little cabbage, a term of endearment usually used by parents for little children. It seemed so totally inappropriate for a man of his dignity that I found it amusing. After all his years alone since his wife had left him, twenty years before, something inside Serge was touched and pleased by this intimacy. "Oh," he would cry out in surprise when I spoke to him in this way. "*Non, c'est amusant*. Continue; I like it."

There was one odd thing about Serge's body. Through the fleshy part of his left upper arm was a hole. The wound itself was long healed, but a small indentation tunneled through the tender flesh. Serge explained that during the war, he had been a freedom fighter. One day out in the Breton woods, a Nazi bullet had come his way. That was all he would say. He quickly changed the subject whenever I mentioned it and pulled away when I touched his arm.

Mid-mornings, we walked together through the enormous gardens, collecting vegetables for the soup that Serge made for lunch. The pink, towered castle that dated from the fifteenth century fascinated me. It was really a miniature château but was still a building of considerable size. Serge used it only for storage as it needed much restoration within to be habitable. "I would love to see the inside of the tower," I remarked.

The heavy wooden stairs, which curved up to the second story, were indented from centuries of footsteps. Because most of the windows were barely more than slits through the deep walls, fortress-like, it was dark, and we had to grope our way along. At the top, an enormous room contained piles of boxes and, surprisingly, a rowboat. "Ah, yes, these are my books from earlier times. I no longer read these sorts of books. Now I have much work to do, much to study."

"What do you mean?"

"My work with the gypsies; I'll tell you about it some other time. Oh, my, yes, *amusant, un bateau dans une tour, n'est-ce pas?*" Isn't it amusing, a boat in a tower?

Serge changed the subject. The large, unfinished room was like a room in a dream, its ancient rafters dusty, strung with cobwebs. Hundreds of boxed books surrounded the very landlocked boat. One end of the room led into the circular tower. The ancient planks sank slightly as we moved about. From the windows of the tower, I could see almost three-hundred-sixty degrees around—over the trout ponds, forests, pink water-mill cottage, the flower and vegetable gardens.

"Why don't you come live here? You could work up in this tower. I would restore it for you. You could even have a horse. The riding is excellent through the woods around here." As always, I loved imagining my way into other lives. What peace there was here. And the possibility of real love, companionship, an idyllic life. It would certainly be a leap of faith to give up the life I knew, my work and home, and make a permanent move to a new country at this point in my life. Would I feel like Rapunzel if I accepted?

"*On va voir.* I'll need to think about it," I said as I hugged him.

A few days after our visit to the tower room, during lunch outside in the garden, I asked, "What is this about the gypsies?" He poured some more wine into each of our glasses.

"Part of every year I spend down near Avignon *avec les gitanes*, with the gypsies. I help to teach the gypsy children. I play my guitar. I live with them for a few weeks at a time. And I bring them to. . . . a better way."

"What do you mean?"

"Him." He pointed overhead to the Breton sky. Over the last years, he explained, he had fully embraced Catholicism. "Oh, yes, it's very helpful, very helpful." When we went inside, he showed me a current pamphlet from the Catholic Church. "It guides me away from offensive or troubling books, movies, and television programs—those that are disturbing to my beliefs."

Gradually, I was becoming aware that Serge was perhaps only being patient with me, waiting for the best moment to push me toward religion. Those outside of Christianity or Judaism were, he felt, lost. One afternoon as we walked past an old synagogue in a small French village, he asked me if I wanted to enter, referring to my Jewish heritage. "You should try," he said. "After all, you are among the chosen people."

Some months later back in the States as I was sitting in a Berkeley café, describing Serge and the hole in his arm, a Jewish friend remarked, "You know, Nazi sympathizers were sometimes identified with such marks." He didn't say how he knew this. Was there a connection between Serge's Catholic work and some hidden guilt concerning his activities during the war?

When I criticized Le Pen, the infamous radical right-wing politician, to Serge, he said he agreed with Le Pen's "*La France pour les Français*" (France for the French) and had voted for him in the last election. "Did you know,"

I teased, "that Le Pen's ex-wife has revealed in the press that he bleaches his hair blond to look more Aryan?"

"*Arrête*. No politics, no religion. Remember?"

The summer was coming to an end. On one of the last days before I left for the States, we drove to the coast and visited old fishing villages. The late-summer sun shone its false promise. After a lunch of wine-soaked mussels, we felt very relaxed and almost groggy as we strolled around the port. These ancient harbors were like museums for the rotting old carcasses of well-used fishing boats. The gray weathered wood revealed the ribs and core of the vessels. Looking inside them felt almost illicit. Once I had had a dream in which I was invited to look inside myself and could hear, see, and feel the sounds and sights of my internal organs at work. Looking into these old boats reminded me of that dream. Somehow, the whole experience was beginning to feel like a waking dream.

"I want to show you the marshlands while the tide is out," Serge said. From where we left the car, we had to walk a long way to reach even an inch or two of sea. The seaweed formed slippery, brown, changing patterns as the tide began to come in. At the bottom of some cliffs, there was enough depth to swim. Serge had carried our swimsuits and towels in a small bag. The water was very cold. "I bathe here most of the year," Serge said as he plunged in. After a very brief dip, I climbed to the top of the cliff.

There they were, just as I had seen them in archaeological photos. In large concentric circles stood the menhirs, ancient and mysterious stones from before the time of the druids. Some of them were etched with vulvas and breasts. What kind of a civilization had lived here? Until recently, no one had paid much attention to the female aspects of this early culture. My own work had moved toward the study of women in ancient cultures. So far, I had not been able to get Serge to be curious about or even accept the validity of such a pursuit. "If I were a geologist studying stones, you would respect that," I said to him.

"That is totally different. That is science. This, what you talk about, is. . . . ah, come on. Remember, no politics, no religion," he reiterated.

Maybe he was right; perhaps I was proselytizing him even as I objected to his efforts to draw me toward Judeo-Christian religious beliefs. Gradually, I hoped, he would respect and show interest in what I did. I touched the stones gently and lay on my back among them, staring up at the clouds, which were starting to blow in rather rapidly.

"Hurry. The tide's coming back," Serge called. I clambered back down to the flats. Serge took my hand and, as the water started up our ankles, we began to run. I had never seen a tide come in so rapidly. The sound of the gurgling, rushing water was hypnotic. I looked ahead to where our car was parked at the top of a cliff. It was at least a mile away. Serge was certainly in better shape than I—he ran easily, and I was already winded. It was thrilling to be swept along at the edge of a natural pattern in this way.

Soon another pattern swept me back to California: teaching commitments, my other life. Always, there was that questioning edge. Like the sea brink where the waves approach and recede, whispering backward off the beach. I pictured life out of time: writing in Serge's tower, walks among the tide pools of Brittany. Would I begin growing my hair long, planning an escape from that charming captivity? And Serge, a reincarnation of a medieval prince, drawn to a modern woman. While Serge drew me out of my world into the peace and rhythm of tides and harvest, I drew him into the pleasures of the body, which he had long denied himself. Perhaps he was beginning to question some of his rigid views. For each of us, these challenges, while intriguing, might prove more than we could bear. Yet the promise of love, home, a coming to rest, a real rest, arms to entwine and comfort: These longings were of course within each of us.

Seven years passed. Work, travel, family deaths occupied me. Serge and I spoke from time to time, wrote perhaps once a year. My mother's death marked the end of my now totally dwindled family. His words: "Don't forget me too soon. *Je vous adresse trois pensées* without limit: *Promesse Tendresse Caresses.*" Later: "Charming and Sexy Lady: I love the seascape of San Francisco that you sent me. I send you a compass to help you negotiate in the fogs which must be quite bad there. . . . Let me hear from you. I hope to have news soon of your return to France. . . . Your P.C." (*petit chou* or little cabbage). I understood that his gift of a compass implied that his views were more clear-sighted than mine.

Something made me pick up the phone and dial Serge's number. A woman answered, apparently a servant. "I will ask *Monsieur le Baron* if he can come to the phone."

"It's you? No, no. I am sick. Don't call me anymore."

Stunned, I hung up the phone. Was he really ill? I sensed some anger in him, a disappointment with me.

Later that summer, I visited friends in their farmhouse in Lussan, in the south of France. With the self-assurance and intuitiveness of a French woman in affairs of the heart, my friend, when she heard about the latest installment in the Serge story, said simply: "You must write him immediately. Don't refer to the phone call."

Within two days, a response to my letter was in my friend's mailbox. "My Fairy Lady. Come to me as soon as you can."

Two trains later, I stepped out onto the quay at St. Amboise des Bois. I felt excited and a bit nervous. Like a slow-motion film, Serge and I ran toward each other from opposite ends of the train platform. His face had a few new lines, but he appeared to be healthy and trim. "You look wonderful, even younger and more beautiful," he said, still the charming Frenchman. "Hurry. We must get home. The haying must be done today, and I have no help, can't afford to hire anyone. Anyway, no one works properly. I must do everything myself."

Later, at lunch, Serge looked at me: "When I saw you last, you seemed more confused. You had some deep unhappiness inside your soul. Now you seem calmer." He continued: "There is a part of you I detest, a part of you I like, a part of you I love. This continues to be the case."

He was in a pensive mood as he apparently had been so often in recent years. He began to play his guitar for me and to sing. I loved the sound of the music and the French language, but his religious songs made me uncomfortable. "What about some Jacques Prévert?" I asked. He switched easily to French love songs.

"You warm my body and my soul, my love." That particular song, its deep tones and eternal longing, always made me shiver. He placed his guitar to one side and looked off into the distance. "It was so odd, you know, I had my small heart attack in the place where we swam together near those old stones. Fortunately, some people were walking along the beach and pulled me out.

"I want to tell you the real story about the hole in my arm. During the war, I was very much in love with a woman who lived in Paris. I was sent off to the German front. I realized I should have proposed marriage to her before I left because I knew there was another man; he was there in Paris. Of course, I couldn't just leave my squadron. So, I shot myself in my upper arm. I had intended it to be just a graze, but I misjudged my aim. The result was a serious wound. But it did give me a medical leave, which had been my intent all along."

"So did you go to her?"

"Yes. But as I had feared, she had already accepted

the other man's offer of marriage. It was one of the great sadnesses of my life. *Je n'ai pas eu de la chance dans ma vie.* So much has not gone right in my life." He recounted a litany of situations gone awry throughout the years.

A few days later, we had dinner at the Coast of the Rose Granite. Le Granit Rose was a place I had loved years before. The sun set behind the small island just off the coast, outlining a small château with gold and rosy hues. As we walked along the coast, Serge said, "Those stupid pagan stones. Let's go in to dinner." In the restaurant, he complained about the slowness of the service. "I have my three-minute rule. If they do not come to us in three minutes, I get up and leave."

The next morning was Sunday, and I suggested we visit some of the Breton "pardon" festivals that were occurring. Religious in origin, these festivals were now a mixture of good times, ancient dances, and traditional foods, such as crunchy Breton waffles. At the town of Guingamp, women strolled in long black embroidered dresses wearing elegant starched lace caps. Dignified men in black suits, some with beards or mustaches, stood about. Soon, the main parade would make its way through the town.

Serge parked on a side street across a large square from the main gathering place. As he turned off the ignition, an urge welled up in me: a sexual urge as well as, perhaps, a desire to test my own power. There was something exciting to me about the mingling of ancient earth religions counterpointed by the repression of them by modern Christianity. Both of these forces were so strong within Serge. Unwilling to contain myself, I touched his thigh, then between his legs, and pulled him around me. "My, my," he said in not unwelcome surprise. Tightening my upper thighs around his, I pressed myself against him. We both rocked and moaned our way to satisfaction. Intermingling with our cries were the ancient strains of Breton music—flutes and drums and bagpipes. Grinning, I looked at him. He pulled himself back together. "Ah, what tedious music. Let's hope no one has seen us. Come, we shall miss the parade. You know this is a very sacred religious gathering." It seemed appropriate that we had made love in the car next to a festival that combined the very elements that were the stuff of the attraction and conflict between Serge and me.

Back on his estate that evening, I watched two doves on the roof outside edge closer together. The breeze that came in tasted of autumn. *L'heure bleue.* Dusk was all around me. In the morning, fog covered northern Brittany. "*La brume est arrivée hier soir* (the fog arrived last evening)," Serge said. All was fog and mist as I looked out—it was like gazing down upon a great cloud. No more green land, no sea.

I needed to think about what to do.

I decided to return home.

From San Francisco, I wrote Serge, suggesting that, before it was too late, why not come together as best we could, share those parts of our lives that we could, give each other love and comfort? The years were passing. I recalled someone once telling me the story of a tired Amazon who decides to take off her armor and rest, but she discovers that it has become attached to her skin. I didn't want this to happen to me.

About ten days later, through my mail slot tumbled a very large and full envelope. Opening it, I found a postcard photo of *la côte de granit rose*. Taped to the back of the card was the Christian credo's "profession of faith": "*Voici ce que je crois*. This is what I believe. It is for me the most important thing in the world. It is totally and absolutely incompatible with your own beliefs. No more projects between us appear to be possible. *Oublie-moi*. Forget me. S." I poured the envelope's contents onto the table. Ten years of my letters and writing lay before me.

Perhaps I always knew that I was pushing him too far, pressing the passions of ancient memories into his own beliefs. It was precisely this conflict that had been enacted on this land as the ancient stones and temples of the earth goddess were toppled by the new religions.

How would Rapunzel have felt if, when she finally let down her hair, the prince tried to cut it off? A kind of reincarnation of a medieval prince with antiquated ideals, not fitting into any world, Serge was left alone, which is perhaps where he always wanted to be. And I had free-fallen into a sea where love and freedom were on opposite shores. We had both drifted out on a tide that had no ebb.

Saved by Colette: Seduction in St. Tropez

"COME SEE MY YACHT," HE SAID

One autumn evening in a restaurant beside the harbor in off-season St. Tropez, I sat eating mussels from a large silver bucket. Two tables away, a handsome and dignified man was similarly sucking the soft bodies from their shells into his mouth. We observed each other licking butter and garlic from our fingers. Blond, silver-streaked hair hung oddly, somehow too evenly, across his forehead. He and the waiter joked back and forth. Apparently, he was a regular patron. When he smiled, something lurked just underneath the gentle spread of his lips: the hint of a sneer, perhaps?

Beside my plate sat Colette's *La Naissance du Jour (Break of Day)*, my dinner companion. I was on a six-month sabbatical from teaching college in Paris where I'd been living for two years and had just attended an international Colette conference in St. Tropez, Colette's home. I was trying to solve a riddle that her writing often tackles: the balancing act between freedom and romantic love, peace of mind and the insistent sexual urges of a middle-aged woman.

Life in France seemed to offer possible solutions to these puzzles. The French accept complex emotions with fewer regrets than most Americans. *C'est la vie* is more than just an expression. They embrace sensuality and enjoy sex like an extension of a good conversation—or meal.

Toward the end of dinner, the waiter approached me. "Monsieur wishes to offer you a cognac."

I nodded.

A large crystal goblet of warmed amber liquid was placed before me. When I raised my glass in acknowledgment to the man sitting at the neighboring table, his blue eyes seemed to spark like a struck flint. His glance shifted almost imperceptibly to my hands, which now cupped the snifter. Then he looked back at my eyes with the slightest hint of amusement. My face heated as I realized that my hands cradled the glass as I might a man's—let me use the French love metaphor—delicacies.

"Madame, would it be too presumptuous on my part if I were to ask to join you at your table? *Je m'appelle Jacques.*"

Our conversation flowed along easily, aided by the comfortable setting, the lovely meal, cognac, and something more: *la seduction*, as the French would say, not referring simply to a direct and perhaps crude sensual drive but rather a central lubricant of life—the tantalizing impossibility of ever quite comprehending the otherness of the man, of the woman. Perhaps it is a metaphor for the destined final futility of getting inside the other's skin. Enter as we will through as many of the body's apertures as possible, still we remain—solidly alone.

I learned that Jacques had lived in St. Tropez much of his life. Sailing was one of his passions, and he would be hosting the judges for the Festival of the Tall Masts, an international gathering of antique sailing vessels from around the world that would begin within a few days.

"Perhaps you would like to watch the competition from my yacht. All the judges will be sailing with me."

I found myself staring at his thumb. There are many ways of sizing up the measure of a man. For me, the thumb never fails. His thumb was broad, moderately long, but its breadth and overwhelming sturdiness and girth were—breathtaking. I had to remind myself to exhale.

"It is still quite early. If you have no pressing plans, I could show you around the harbor. We could stroll over to my yacht."

Its name, *La Hurlette*, was intriguing. It translated as "The Screamer." The soft dark navy-blue velvet of the cushioned cabin and the lapping Mediterranean outside eased the tightness in my shoulders. The slight night breeze off the water caused a chill to tide over my skin, contrasting to the warmth that was flowing down my spine, down to my thighs, increasing the tingling and throbbing between my legs. With a sweep of hand, Jacques offered me a seat on one of the boat's couches. He sat across the cabin from me. He spoke in a serious, calm tone as I expected more details about the upcoming sailing competition.

Instead, he looked firmly and directly at me.

"I would like to kiss you all over your entire body, lick between your toes, behind your ears—no, not yet there. First I will tease you, massage your thighs with my hands. Do you like a bit of strong pressure? I think you do. Finally, my tongue will visit your sex, will delicately—oh, so delicately taste its way between your legs. No, I don't want you to open up too soon, not too soon. My tongue, my lips, will find your soft folds, your *chat*. You will help me to know what is best and better for you with your moanings, your cries, soft at first and then. . . . we shall see, won't we?"

From my own field research, it did seem that French lovers are more verbal than their American counterparts, and Jacques was no exception.

Opposite him, I found it increasingly difficult to sit upright on the yacht's soft cushions. Already he had moved inside me even from that distance, and I was inside his voice, wondering how he would look, smell, taste. Still, we were both fully clothed and watching each other from a distance.

"Shall I undress you now? Are you ready for me to kiss you everywhere? I mean really everywhere? In places you perhaps have not been caressed before? Will you be ready for that?"

He moved closer to me, helped me to my feet. He unbuttoned the top buttons of my thin summer blouse. I wanted only to open up and have him pleasure me. Quickly now, he pulled off my clothes; somehow while my eyes were closed for a moment, he became naked. He was a tall man, athletically built. The slightest hint of thickening girth reflected years of sensual pleasure at the table, and the firmness of his torso and thighs affirmed sensuality of a different nature.

Then we were in the king-sized bed in the master cabin with its navy-blue sheets. The lapping water and the soft breeze of the *Midi* tickled my heated body. He slipped his body around and let my lips find his engorged cock. It was what the French call *gros*. The intended meaning is "thick" rather than large. Somehow, the word *gros* itself always excited me. To pronounce it correctly, one's mouth has to move in three small syllables. The impetus of the word has to begin deep in your throat. Just saying "grow" makes me feel like I am preparing my throat to open up, to absorb one of the thickest cocks imaginable.

As he entered me, I entered him. Our waves moved in and out of each other. I floated into the zone that is beyond thought and focus. As I was on the edge of coming, he pulled out of me, lifted me backward so that my head was just hanging off the edge of the bed. Now he dived into me with his flickering tongue.

"*Non, non*, not yet," he intoned.

He stroked me with his words, which flowed over me continually. "*C'est gross, ma bite. C'est vrai, n'est pas? Tu est mouillé, totallement mouillé. Tu vas jouir, oui?*"

Part of the charm of French is that it sounds so good even if you don't understand everything fully.

The French words for wet and for orgasm are onomatopoetic. "Wet," *mouillé*, requires a pursing of the lips and then a release like a waterslide "eeeee." "I come," *je jouie*, is a different type of contraction. "Je" and "joo" plus "oui" form a gigantic affirmation: "OUI."

During the next week or so, I stayed at Jacques' house, sailing whenever I chose with him and the officials of the competition during the day. However, as absorbed and dedicated a lover as he was, in public he was like a ship in dry-dock. And in everyday matters, he was abrupt, even rude. At his house, when we were not making love, he seemed to forget I was there.

One night, saddened by his coldness, I checked back into my hotel. My woman's body and soul had been penetrated fully by this man. Yet he never offered romantic love. Here was an offer of total freedom and passion and pleasure but I found it wanting. I drove up to Colette's house, la Treille Muscate, which perched on a hill above the town at the end of a narrow country road. For a while, I sat in the garden outside her yellow home and looked down at the bay. On the porch, a young woman was engrossed in her writing. Wandering the old gardens, which are open to visitors, I felt my calm and peacefulness return.

Each day now, the restaurants were closing for the winter. The nights were chill; leaves were blowing in yellow and orange clouds on the *pétanque* court in the square in front of my hotel. One night, I went for dinner at the restaurant where I had met Jacques. It was almost empty. The waiter told me this was their last night of the season.

The next morning I packed, putting my bags in the trunk of my Renault. I opened the sunroof to better enjoy the autumn sun and blue sky. Checking my map, I picked out the route that would take me along the *calanche* to Antibes and later Menton. For a moment, I looked in the rearview mirror at the reflection of the landscape where I had been. Then I put the car into gear and hugged the curves overlooking the luscious Mediterranean. I punched the record button on my tape recorder and began to tell the story of my time that autumn in St. Tropez.

Diving Deep and Letting Go in Egypt

How I Forgot to Visit the Sphinx

We have lingered in the chambers of the sea
By sea-girls wreathed in seaweed red and brown
Till human voices wake us, and we drown.

"The Love Song of J. Alfred Prufrock"—T. S. Eliot

It was shark breeding season. On my first dive in the Red Sea off the Sinai Peninsula near Sharm el-Sheikh, we watched fifteen ten-foot black-tip male sharks circle one black-tip female. As a single female from San Francisco, I was amazed at the sight of fifteen males devoting their total attention to one female. She seemed to ignore them and go about her business, poking in and out of crevices, which appeared to be the shark equivalent of running errands.

I was giving myself a Christmas/winter solstice gift of two weeks' rest and diving aboard the *Lady Jenny IV,* an English-owned and operated dive boat. It was part of a month-long trip to Egypt, a break from an unusually icy winter in Paris where I was living the expat American life and teaching.

Relaxing on the deck between dives, I was lulled by the Sinai, the islands of the Red Sea, the sea itself. Most predominant was the simplicity of its colors. In the near and far distance lay the land—barren with gradations of camel-tan from the palest off-white cream to a darker caramel-colored cafe-au-lait. Yet this same land seen from a distance became layered in a gray-blue haze. It all resembled the straight and curved lines of Arabic script. One saying goes that Arabic is so difficult to interpret that out of three people, one will say its meaning is one thing, another person will interpret the same serpentine scrawl differently, and a third will say it is only the picture of the humps on a camel's back. I turned my attention back to the sea, which we were about to enter.

"Red Sea sharks never bother humans." Despite our English dive guide's reassurance before we'd taken that giant step off the boat into the waters of our first dive, I was amused to notice that when the sharks' mating dance came into view at ninety feet under how we had all, including our guides, unconsciously wended our way behind a flimsy rotting railing on the slanted deck of the wreck we had just begun to investigate. After more than three-hundred hours of diving during the past decade, still the silence, the beauty, and the sense of that slender edge between being alive and being dead amazed me.

Equally stunning is the contrast of surfacing after a dive. Always, I am reluctant to leave the world down there. One moment, weightlessness, the light eternally like a late-afternoon New England autumn, the only sounds one's own inhalations and exhalations. The next moment, after emerging from the clear azure waters, the almost unbearable heaviness of the tank, the awkwardness of the rubber suit and fins. "Hey, Joe, you want a beer?" Loud laughter. The whang of heavy steel tanks being dropped into their holders. In this case, from the grandeur of black-tip shark mating to the smells of crêpes with scrambled eggs and coffee.

Life on a well-organized dive boat is placid, pleasant, and self-contained. We dove before breakfast around 8:30. Thick towels and a hot breakfast awaited us after we returned: cold, waterlogged, and slightly "narced" from the deep. My theory is that the jolly effects of nitrous-oxide absorption contribute more than people realize to the popularity of sport diving. Laughing gas with one-hundred feet of saltwater above you, brilliantly colored swaying vegetation, surrealistic creatures around you, and the weightlessness of an astronaut— who wouldn't want to stay?

Back on deck after breakfast, I soaked up the sun and sights. The sea continued to be absolutely placid. Not many ships come through this area of the Red Sea. It remains largely uncharted. It is of no commercial interest except to dive boats, and with the continuing military skirmishes in the area, fewer and fewer of these. We cruised in and out among many small islands, most of them mined and inhabited, if at all, only by Egyptian military bases. The undulating land in its variegated browns caught and reflected the blue of the water in pockets of shadow. Like a photographic negative, the blue water mirrored the sandy lines of the dunes.

Tomorrow I'd be leaving this peaceful life and taking the bus back to Cairo, where I had promised Hassan I would meet his family. My desire to be a fly on the wall in as many locations as possible sometimes overcomes any better judgment. Hassan, an educated, unmarried man, was my archaeological guide when I first arrived in Egypt. During my time in Cairo a few weeks earlier, we had enjoyed getting to know each other. He had taken me to all the typical sites, including a visit to King Tut's treasures, racing Arab horses together at sunset over the dunes near the Sphinx at Giza, shopping for a cartouche with my name engraved, and eating in tiny local restaurants on the outskirts of Cairo. Traveling on my own for the first time in Egypt, it was a treat to have my own local escort.

Never interested in being just a tourist, I was fascinated to sink into the life here, and began my pattern as a single traveler of having a lover here and there as a perfect way to experience a people and their culture. A love affair with an interesting local person offered me a suitable escort, fun companionship, and sex, and allowed me to see deeper into a culture.

As a curious traveler, I always welcome unusual experiences as they add spice to my adventure. For example, after we dismounted from our horses near the pyramids, Hassan suggested we have a look inside a small nearby tomb. The interior was spacious, if dusty.

My loose overblouse and dark billowy trousers felt at home in the ancient gloom and were very flexible. But it was a time-travel experience to imagine all the people who had inhabited this interior thousands of years earlier. I knew from archaeological excavations that Egyptian beds were not soft like our modern ones, and the ancient tombstone was no exception when we ended up making love inside this structure with its view of the pyramids. During our time there, we felt part of a continuum as we viewed the fish, cattle, and processions of people painted on the walls. Even the painted elaborate golden beds on the walls enticed us as we settled for simpler stone accommodations.

A final irony of this distraction is that I forgot to visit the Sphinx. This had been my original purpose in coming to Egypt.

In previous days, I had spent time with Hassan in his unheated and barely furnished bachelor's apartment in a residential area of Cairo. "Now that I have been able to buy my own place, I am able to marry," he told me. Returning to Cairo, I suspected that according to local custom, we were now engaged. This was a result I hadn't anticipated.

Unlike the stereotypical view of the single woman as passive victim to lusty foreigners, the men I've met in my travels were the unfortunate ones. At least back in those days, before much of the world's population was traveling as a hobby, in many countries, the possibility of an educated and talented man meeting a marriageable woman, especially one as free-spirited, traveled, and sophisticated as I, was slim. In retrospect, I'm sorry if I may have played the unintentional heartbreaker. Like a female Candide, I was curious in researching "the best of all possible worlds." How did diverse human beings figure out how to live the best lives for themselves? But always, I was the observer with the intention of moving on.

Back in Cairo, Hassan met me at the bus station and told me about plans to introduce me to his family.

Crumbs in an Egyptian Bedroom

How Do YOU Warm Your Biscuits?

In Cairo, on the fifth-floor walkup of a middle-class apartment house, Hassan's mother sat in her bed at 6 p.m., surrounded by her two adult sons and daughter. The stairs on our way up were lined with garbage: overflowing bags as well as loose bottles, cans, rinds, gnawed bones. In the bedroom was a large four-poster bed with soiled sheets. Hassan's mother sat upright at the head of the bed like an empress receiving her courtiers. She wore a headdress, or turban, which at some point had been white. It was now a gray-and-brown-streaked smoky smear. A similarly unsavory off-white flannel nightgown glued itself sweatily to various parts of her body because of the smoldering Egyptian heat. It clung especially to her pendulous breasts and stuck between her buttocks when, with the aid of her sons, she arose from her bed. She moved out of her bed in order to change her headdress in my honor.

When she removed herself from the bed, the rumpled dirty sheets, damp with human secretions and streaked with long gray hairs, were revealed to be nesting about ten biscuits. Hassan's mother had baked a large bucket of hard Egyptian biscuits, I was told, that afternoon in preparation for my visit. While waiting for my arrival with her son Hassan, she had apparently amused herself by munching on these biscuits, and the ten had escaped and found their way to nestle under her ample buttocks where they became moist and warm. While she was freshening her turban, her attentive sons scooped the biscuits up off the mattress and placed them carefully on her nightstand beside the biscuit bucket. When Hassan's mother returned to her former position in the bed and we were all summoned to snuggle up comfortably around her on the bed to share the evening supper, she began, with great affection, to feed me the wayward biscuits, one after another, that were now on the night table. They were moist and warm but flavorful. After two biscuits, I feigned a feminine sign of being satiated as I strained to continue acting my role as honored potential family member.

    Hassan touched my hand possessively and with awareness: "My sister will come to visit you in Paris. It would be good for her. She must get out more if she is to find a husband." Hassan and I conversed in a mixture of German and French. He translated for his family and me. His twenty-two-year-old sister sat close beside me. All of us—Hassan's mother, brother, sister, Hassan, and I—sat in a variety of cross-legged or reclining positions on Hassan's mother's big rumpled bed. We shared the evening meal Middle Eastern-style. Hassan did the cooking: scrambled eggs, a kind of greasy-looking pastrami, and some vegetables and spices. He placed the large frying pan in the center of the bed. Using only our fingers, we all dipped into it with pieces of flatbread. *At least this course is heated on the stove and not by Hassan's mother's rump,* I thought.

Hassan insisted on feeding me, with his fingers, some choice bits from the pan. Our bed companions all gazed at me with warmth. The assumption was that Hassan was now engaged to an American woman who was to be treated as part of the family. I relaxed into the loving and cozy feeling around me. It felt strange to me, someone pretty much without any close kin for many years now, who lived a kind of vagabond life. Freedom sometimes had its downside. Here was an extremely attractive, intelligent, interesting, and kind man. He had a significant library in his apartment, and we had enjoyed discussing some of the few writers we both knew. I wanted to know more about Naguib Mahfouz's writing and political problems. Winner of the Nobel Prize, he was constantly harassed because of his political views, even fearing for his life. "You can get a job at the American University. I have some contacts there," Hassan had told me. It was all very tempting.

His sister tugged on my arm: "I want to show you something," she whispered. She was a sweet, pretty young woman who, even though she attended law school, felt uncomfortable going to the cinema on her own.

"She can go out with friends, I tell her, but she just stays here in the apartment when she is not at law school," Hassan complained.

"It is up to my brothers to find me a husband. I don't like to go out. But I would go to Paris with you."

I thought about the contradictions, at least to the Western mind, of studying law and at the same time following traditional Egyptian female patterns of behavior. Of course, I could sympathize that the sandy, surly streets of Cairo weren't a whole lot of fun to stroll around on your own as a single woman. However, I worried about having this girl appear on the doorstep of my Paris apartment. I changed the subject. "What are your favorite subjects? Tell me more about your friends at the university."

She frowned at my request and pushed her photo album into my lap. It apparently was a proud summary of her life so far, displaying a few photos from a family wedding and several birthday parties. I stared at the yet-to-be-filled blank pages. Enough of the conversation came through to me: Plans were being made for my future sister-in-law to come stay with me in Paris during our engagement. I smiled sweetly and, with my hand in the deep pocket of my favorite black traveling jacket, secretly fondled my plane ticket to Luxor, my next stop —and wondered if there were any flights the next day.

As soon as it seemed acceptable, after extensive thank-you's and many hugs all around, I excused myself due to fatigue and asked Hassan to please drive me back to my hotel. I promised him that I would call when I knew the date of my return flight from Luxor and Aswan. That all seemed to be something to think about in the future. Meanwhile, I was ready for New Year's, when I could visit the ruins of Luxor and explore farther south on the Nile at Aswan.

An Unexpected New Year's Eve in Luxor

Testing Egyptian Machismo

On New Year's Eve in the working-class residential section of Luxor, Egypt, among muddy alleys and run-down tenements, I sat in the center of a small living room. Gathered around me were six young Egyptian men smoking hashish through a hookah. My fitted white St. Tropez skirt and flowing light-green silk blouse were so uncommon here that I felt almost like an untouchable. *Sort of like reverse nun wear,* I thought. My escort, a man I had met in my hotel lounge a few days before, was an archaeological guide, an occupation that seemed to be ubiquitous for young unmarried Egyptian men with some education. He and I spoke French, and he acted as translator.

The pouring rain had continued since I'd arrived in Luxor a few days before from Cairo. I was traveling by public bus around Egypt, roundtrip through the Sinai to Sharm el-Sheikh for a dive trip, and then back to Cairo, the hub for any public transportation. Small airports did not yet exist in many places in this country. Traveling by bus enabled me to see more of the country and meet everyday Egyptian people more easily, although few women rode on the buses at the time. A few months earlier in St. Tropez where I was on sabbatical from teaching in Paris, I'd been introduced to the owner of an excellent English tourism company. When I mentioned my interest in visiting Egypt, he offered to arrange my trip. They made top-notch arrangements for me, including reasonably priced luxury hotels.

Checking into the Winter Palace in Luxor—Agatha Christie's home, where she composed *Death on the Nile*—I unwound into the warmth and golden splendor. The hotel, built in 1886, exuded colonial extravagance with twinkling chandeliers, elaborate Egyptian-themed draperies and carpets, and attendants and waiters who pampered the fortunate clientele, including me.

Settling into my opulent room, I looked out at the Nile flowing past and wondered if perhaps Agatha Christie had looked out this very window and was inspired by the view. I was very excited to be in the heart of ancient Thebes, Luxor's original name. As a professor of world literature, I had imagined life in this ancient city through the references in Homer's *Iliad* and Sophocles' *Oedipus Rex* and *Antigone*. In the *Iliad*, Book 9 (c. eighth century BCE), Homer extols the city's opulence: ". . . . in Egyptian Thebes the heaps of precious ingots gleam, the hundred-gated Thebes."

I dressed for the evening and went downstairs for cocktails and dinner. While I was relaxing in the lounge, a young man introduced himself as Ahmed, an archaeological guide. After we talked for a while, he asked if I had arranged my visit yet and offered to guide me around the Valley of the Kings and Queens during my stay. The following evening there, the opera *Aida* would be performed in its very setting of Karnak. "If you are interested," Ahmed said, "I can purchase tickets for us and we can attend the performance after touring the tombs and monuments tomorrow." This sounded perfect, and I accepted.

Early the following morning, Ahmed picked me up at my hotel and we traveled to the West Bank across the Nile for explorations of the famous tombs. Lots of hiking in the continuing drizzle, amazing descents into darkened passageways, so many wall inscriptions to study—it was like ingesting hundreds of history books in a single day. I especially enjoyed trying to sink back into the consciousness of these tomb inhabitants by studying the images on the walls that depicted their selected necessities for the next life: foods, amphorae of drinks, animals (especially cats), carriages, slaves, servants, and of course, gods. There they were as companions into eternity: the falcon-headed Horus; Hathor with her headdress of cow horns and sun disk; Osiris, god of fertility and the dead; and their many colleagues. *Maybe it would be comforting to believe in such a detailed next life,* I thought, but really found it impossible to imagine. I have enough trouble packing for a few weeks' trip and couldn't imagine packing for eternity, although I suppose all those slaves and gods would be helpful.

After a short rest back at the Winter Palace, I met Ahmed, and along with thousands of spectators, we picked our way past the Avenue of the Sphinxes through muddy alleys to our seats facing the Nile beside the Temple of Karnak. Fortunately, by the time we set out, the rains had subsided.

After a magnificent performance in this four-thousand-year-old Theban temple—during which I admit to dozing off a bit, one of the hazards of intense days on the road as a traveler and a long day exploring the tombs—Ahmed accompanied me back to the Winter Palace, where we had dinner. I enjoyed watching my first authentic belly dancing performance, realizing that classic belly dancers do, indeed, sport fleshy bellies. No anorexia in their ranks.

During dinner, Ahmed talked about other American women tourists he'd guided, asked about my plans, and invited me, if I were free, the next evening to join him at a New Year's Eve party at his local friends' apartment. He spoke French well and was witty, educated, and well-mannered. This sounded like fun as well as an opportunity to experience more of the real Luxor.

The following evening around 9 p.m., we met in the hotel lobby, where we chatted for a while about our lives and interests. Time flew as we conversed about tourists and guides, relationships and chance meetings. Ahmed cut my musing short. "*On y va*," Ahmed said suddenly. "We must go, or we'll be late."

In front of the hotel, he flagged down a *calèche*, or horse-drawn taxi, the main mode of transportation in Luxor at the time. The short trip afforded me a glimpse of life away from the tourist center and hotels as we made our way into the working-class residential section. People and horses struggled for space along the eerily dark streets. One half-starved horse had lost her footing and kneeled on the slippery street. Its owner beat the poor animal with a whip, but there seemed no solution. They were both stuck. I yelled out at the man to stop. Having trained and ridden horses for many years, seeing this mare mistreated was painful to me. Somehow, the scene reminded me of some of the travelers Ahmed and I had discussed, women who like Emma Bovary were bored with their lives back home, who imagined they were in love with him, and who fantasized about moving to Egypt to begin a new life with him. Perhaps they felt equally helpless and stuck in the figurative mud. We drove on.

    Our carriage came to a stop in front of a simple tan stucco apartment house, drying wash hanging out of windows and merchants with carts hawking goods in the street. Ahmed took my arm and we escaped the hubbub into the building, and then walked up two flights of dimly lit stairs. The whole experience was both exciting and a bit overwhelming as I moved into a truly foreign world. Entering Ahmed's friend's flat, we met six young Egyptian men who were gathered around a hookah, smoking hashish. He introduced me as an American professor and writer from San Francisco and Paris. They took a break from their refreshment to stand and greet me politely, if with some curiosity and awkwardness on both our sides. The men were a bit younger than Ahmed, probably in their late thirties, dressed casually in jeans, cotton shirts, and sweaters. One by one, each of the young men shook my hand in a formal manner. Teachers and professors are well respected in this culture. After a while, they invited me to share their hookah, which I did. It helped ease any cross-cultural tensions. Their sisters, wives, and girlfriends peered in from the kitchen doorway and smiled timidly.

Tarek, the host, offered me a seat on an upholstered chair in the center of the small living room. Conversation moved slowly as all comments had to be translated by Ahmed into French for me, and my remarks had to be repeated in Arabic for the others. They asked about what life was like in the USA, about my students, and about what I thought of Egypt. "I'm traveling alone to do research for my classes and my writing," I explained. This partly eased their curiosity about a single woman traveling by herself in their culture.

"This is a new experience for them," Ahmed explained. "They have never been in such an intimate setting with a non-Egyptian woman before."

While I chatted with the young men, their wives and female relatives remained clustered in the kitchen, cooking. Intermittently, they brought salads, meats, and pastries into the room, where they placed them on the center table and then left without a word. I tried to make eye contact with them, asking Ahmed to translate for me. "What is your name?" "You are very pretty." "How do you make that dish?" Each answered shyly, lowering their dark lashes and turning away before returning to the kitchen, where I could hear giggles and soft conversation.

After a couple of hours visiting, eating, and sharing our ideas for the new year, we all rose to leave. One of the young men I'd been chatting with offered to show me his new apartment. "I recently bought it and would be proud to show you. It took me a long time to save the money," he said.

"Of course," I replied without hesitation. "I'd be honored." Along with Ahmed, we walked to where his new apartment was, up a dark, sticky flight of stairs. As we climbed, fatigue from the long day suddenly hit me, and I had second thoughts about what I was doing. Why was I going to look at the empty apartment of someone I had just met? But it was too late to backtrack, so I followed them up the stairs. He unlocked the door and we entered a darkened, sparsely furnished flat. It smelled of dampness and wet plaster. In the gloom, I could make out one chair, a small table, and a single unmade bed. The man in whose apartment we stood closed the door behind us and squared his shoulders as he said, "Aren't you worried about your safety coming into a place like this with two men?"

I had thought about this. Curiosity often drew me into these situations. How far could I push the experience? I really wasn't afraid at all. Actually, I had always been more leery of being trapped in the traditional woman's life of my era—at home, dependent, with a husband and children—than I was when free to follow my curiosity on the road.

When I wonder about my comfort with risk-taking, sometimes I attribute it to having a lot of training and experience in dealing with challenging situations:

Working with horses for many years as a show-horse trainer, backpacking in the wilderness, and scuba diving have all nurtured a kind of self-discipline. There's no point screaming when a horse falls on top of you or your dive regulator gets stuck on a wall in the dark and you're trapped in a cave under one-hundred feet of water. You take a deep breath, stay calm, and figure it out.

Of course, there's the desire for love and intimacy as well as adventure that many of us share. These urges cause some of us to take all kinds of risks.

Relying on my hopefully untouchable reverse-nun magic mode, I took a deep breath and tried to exude calm. "Of course not," I replied. "With gentlemen like yourselves, I know that I am well protected." The unstated but palpable tension in the room deflated, and we all smiled and made light conversation. Ahmed and I said our farewells, exited, and took a *calèche* back to the Winter Palace, where Ahmed and I said our goodbyes. Walking up the marble hotel stairs and through doors opened by liveried doormen, I returned from one Egyptian world and entered another. Although this was not at all the extreme travels depicted in the tombs—from life to the afterworld—I was still experiencing how different worlds can exist within one culture.

In the morning, on the bus heading to Aswan, my next stop, my heart raced a little when I thought about the possibly risky situation I had been in. Without realizing it, I had appealed to the less recognized side of machismo that involves honor, respect, and nurturance—and it worked. These young men sought my respect and understanding as much as I did theirs. For me, one of the joys of travel is sharing our common humanity, no matter our lack of a common language or culture. This remains a special New Year's Eve memory for me.

Tea on the Nile: Aswan

"I Am Going to Throw," and Other Mistranslations

After weeks of traveling through the Sinai on public buses and wandering through the muddy back streets of Cairo and Luxor, I found myself sitting down to a silver-service afternoon tea in a luxuriant flower garden beside a glittering swimming pool at the Old Cataract Hotel in Aswan. It had been a complicated early-morning flight from Luxor to Aswan. My tired bones and cramped muscles began to relax in the warm late-afternoon sun as I looked out over the gleaming Nile and its graceful feluccas—small, swan-like historic sailing vessels dating from the time of the Pharaohs.

"May I offer you one of these biscuits? They're very special."

I looked up at a distinguished-looking Egyptian man in his late-fifties, smiling and nodding toward me as he offered a small silver tray from his own adjacent tea table. We both sipped hibiscus tea from delicate porcelain cups. The whole setting made me feel like we were all transported back to nineteenth-century colonial England. He introduced himself as Nabil Fakhry. Even though his skin and hair coloring indicated that he was

Egyptian, the gentleman's accent was very Oxford, as was his casual but elegant afternoon dress and demeanor. "The hotel was built in 1899 by Thomas Cook," my new friend informed me. He told me that Agatha Christie's *Death on the Nile* was filmed on these grounds.

His brown eyes, olive skin, and the tweeds he wore spoke to me of eons of history and matched his pipe, which seemed to be a permanent fixture between his full, moist lips. After chatting for some time, I excused myself to return to my room. As I got up to leave, he asked, "Would you like to join me for dinner?" I accepted and we agreed to meet at 7 p.m. in the lobby.

During the following week, Nabil and I became friends and more. We visited coffee houses and restaurants where women normally would not venture. Certainly, it would have been impossible for me to have experienced them alone. Except when he was eating, his pipe remained such a constant feature that I was curious what he did with it during lovemaking and sleep. We were to become close friends over the rest of my time in Aswan, so I had the opportunity to find out.

At the hotel, other distinguished-looking guests showed him much deference. During our chats, I learned that he was a circuit court judge, highly respected and well-known throughout Egypt. "I've given up civil law because I no longer can support laws that allow men to beat and even kill their wives if they suspect them of infidelity," he told me. Recently widowed after a long marriage caring for a chronically ill wife, he was eager to resume a more active life. For me, making the acquaintance of a pro-feminist and intellectual Egyptian male escort was unexpected and a rare gift. Over the next days, we became more intimate. This wasn't that simple due to the customary guard or chaperone on each floor and the necessity of Nabil, because of his high position, not to risk his reputation by being seen coming to my room. Somehow, with much discretion, we worked it out.

Nabil spoke excellent British English with the delightful literal translations from his own language that pop up so amusingly in the speech of most of us who live in more than one language. One example was very comical, especially in retrospect. When he was about to have an orgasm, for example, he would shout: "I am going to throw." The first time I experienced this, I almost jumped back, expecting a pillow or a fragile teacup to sail through the air.

At dinner on the night before I left Aswan to return to Cairo and then Paris, we sat in the soft candlelight of the exquisite Old Cataract Hotel restaurant, the Nile gliding by outside the window. I imagined Agatha Christie or Winston Churchill at neighboring tables.

My judge friend said: "Next summer, I want to travel with you throughout Eastern Europe. I shall give you $3,000, and you will handle all the arrangements. If we get on together, we shall be married. When you return to Paris, you must write me and say, 'I want you, Nabil,' or not. Then I will know what to do."

I was both stunned and intrigued by his proposal. Here was an opportunity for a unique new life. But, as always, I thought about the stability of my own base: my home in San Francisco, my tenured college teaching job, my independence. Of course, the possibility of love and companionship always beckoned me. The privileged and intellectual classes in Egypt live very well. But early-twentieth-century novelist Ellen Glasgow's words were ever in my brain: "Hearts may be broken, men may come and go, but the cows must be milked."

I had to tend to my own "cows."

There were two additional considerations as well. Nabil was a vegetarian and explained to me the process that was necessary to wash all lettuce and vegetables in his home with dish detergent because of the human excrement used as fertilizer. Watching the way he drooled a bit out of the right corner of his moist lips as he smoked his pipe, a vision of me at a kitchen sink in bustling Cairo, far from the loveliness of Aswan, scrubbing an infinite procession of lettuce leaves flowed through my mind. Back in Paris, I began to compose my letter, a gentle but firm "no thanks."

PART III

Taking Chances and New Models

Wild women don't worry
Wild women don't have the blues.
   —Ida Cox, blues singer

An Italian Bedtime Story

Hot Times on an Italian Train

Nothing was moving; everyone seemed stunned. The Berlin Wall had recently come down, and Eastern Europe was like a sea between two tides. It was July 4, 2000, in the midst of World Cup frenzy. Earlier that day, I'd left Prague on a train bound for Rome and then to see friends who lived south of Pompeii. It had taken two days of waiting in long lines to get a plane or train ticket out of Prague.

Now that I was finally on my way, weariness seeped into me, the kind that comes from being on the road, a rather bumpy one, for quite a while. I was returning to Italy. *Bella Italia*. I sighed and relaxed. No more warm milk over boiled potatoes and cabbage. My head was spinning with accounts from Party members who feared they would lose their jobs and so many who longed for some abstract of freedom. My notebook held all their tales, and I looked forward to sorting them out into stories. After the asceticism of Eastern Europe, soon I would be pampered with Italian food, joviality, and gentle landscapes. Comforts awaited me.

The only other person in my train compartment, a

burly fellow in a pale-blue cotton shirt, pulled off his well-worn cap, exposing thinning light-brown hair, and pumped my hand up and down. His vigor was a healthy contrast to our stuffy quarters. "Andrej, *mi piacere*," he said. "I am heading down to the soccer matches. I am coach for the Czechoslovakian team."

So here was a bit of Eastern Europe beginning to spill out from behind the wilted Iron Curtain. Andrej's slightly dazed and pale demeanor reminded me of someone venturing into sunlight after a long illness in a darkened room. Using German as our common language, we discussed bits of our lives. He told me about his work at a small university just outside of Prague. I taught in a college, too, near San Francisco, so we compared our students, discussed our enjoyment of seeing them succeed, and empathized over how frustrating the lazy ones were. I had never thought about physical education teachers at communist universities. Small, glum groups discussing Marxist theory had been my Western-propagandized mental imagery, not fatherly-looking coaches laughing with their students.

"*Ja*, what a hot night!" I agreed, and we each settled into our bunks on opposite sides of the otherwise unoccupied space.

With each passing moment, the unventilated car became ever more sizzling. I dozed fitfully, and at 4 a.m., I finally realized a radiator adjacent to my couchette was on, blasting just beside my right ear. Sweat poured off my body, and I had a terrible headache.

I decided to go against a major commandment when traveling the Italian rails. "Thou shalt keep your door locked, particularly while asleep." *I'm such a light sleeper,* I thought. *If I just slide the door open a bit, I'll get some air. With my purse under my head and my arm resting on my suitcase, I'll be fine.* Andrej was snoring softly as I quietly unlocked and opened our compartment door, then slipped back onto my bunk.

The next thing I knew, I was having one of those dreams in which you try to move but are paralyzed. I managed to raise my heavy eyelids ever so slightly. A nightmarish mirage stunned me.

An angular man backed out of our space, past the sleeping soccer coach, smirking while at the same time nodding reassuringly at me. His glance and raised hand warned: *Don't get up. Don't move. Just lie there.* The man's reddish-hued, elongated face, and lean body had the cast of the devil. Disheveled hair, the color of watery blood, stood up on both sides of his sweaty skull like two horns. I strained to raise my arms, to move my legs. Nothing. Though I was only partially conscious, some reflexive part of my brain told me I had to force myself to grab for my purse. Weakly, I moved my right hand behind my head.

My purse was gone. Just a few moments earlier, my black leather traveling purse had cushioned my head and neck. Securely nested inside the purse—in addition to my wallet, money, credit cards, address book, favorite jewelry, and return ticket to the States—was my notebook from the last four weeks of travel. Stretching my arm and hand back behind my head, I probed again, harder and deeper. Everything had vanished.

Like the Cheshire Cat, the vermilion northern Italian had evaporated along with all my valuables, leaving behind, sizzled into my memory, only his malevolent smirk.

The torridity of the night oozed into every part of my body. "Something really terrible has just happened to me," I murmured to myself. I shook my head, trying to clear my brain. Drugged? Had I been drugged? How?

Andrej had slept through everything. Struggling to reach a standing, if wobbly position, I shouted, hoping he could help me: "I've been robbed!" I tried saying this in English, French, and German. He got the idea and sat up on his bunk, rubbing his eyes with his large fingers.

On trembling knees, balancing myself against the compartment walls as the train jolted along, I tottered out into the train aisle and shouted: "Help, I've been robbed."

"So have we," replied Australian voices. Several young men in jeans were stumbling around in the train aisle. "Someone's got everything. Our musical instruments. We were to give a concert in *Firenze* [Florence]. We're earning our way by playing as we go." Three men in their early twenties stood there, looking helpless. One sobbed: "My only pair of eyeglasses were in my cello case. I can't see without them. All our money's gone."

As we commiserated, we realized we were the victims of a classic Italian train experience, one I'd been warned about: During brief stops at stations, Ferrara en route to Florence in this case, professional thieves board the train and shoot an aerosol chloroform preparation into the compartments, which temporarily paralyzes the occupants. The thieves then grab valuables and jump off the train as it leaves the station, too late for the stunned victims to do anything except wail and get off at the next stop to report their losses to indifferent authorities who hear the same stories every day.

The conductor, who was slinking about, smirked at me. "You have insurance, no? All Americans have insurance. You'll be okay." It dawned on me that he was probably involved in the theft.

"Who do you think put the heat on in the train on such a beastly hot night?" I said to the Australians.

"Righto," said the calmest of the Australians, "and we unsuspecting foreigners opened our compartment doors for a little breath of air."

My adrenaline-fueled blood pressure made my head want to explode. I needed to act. Insisting the conductor go with me, we inspected the trash in every toilet on the train. Although I was pretty sure my purse was long gone, I wanted to annoy him as much as possible.

As the train pulled into the Rome station, Andrej turned to me. "I would like to help you out and give you some money," he said, "but you know we don't have credit cards yet in Eastern Europe, and my foreign currency is really limited, but here's what I can spare. It's not much." He handed me ten-thousand lire, enough for a sandwich and drink. I had another six hours of travel ahead of me. He was meeting his team in Italy and kept only a few thousand lire for himself. The conductor was holding my passport and ticket, which would get me to my friends in the south.

That was it. As we said goodbye, I choked back tears, reluctant to leave this small connection with a kinder world.

"You must take me to the police station," I told the conductor, who was looking sheepish. I tried to make my five-foot-two inches as tall and my voice as assertive as possible. I was afraid that if the conductor didn't accompany me to the police office in the cavernous Rome train station, I'd lose my way and miss my connection to southern Italy. If that happened, I had no money to buy an additional ticket. Also, I was still floating in the ether of illusion that often helps us puny humans through crummy experiences. Somehow, I thought reporting the theft might magically cause my personal belongings, especially my notebook, to be returned to me.

Inside the humid, rancid-smelling police office, about one-hundred angry people pushed and shouted, trying to get the attention of a bald sweating man with a badge. The mob seemed, like me, to be foreigners who had been robbed. We all filled out forms and pressed toward the front, where the man was stamping papers.

The officer looked at my papers and up at me. Then he scrunched up his dripping face and started winking at me. For a moment, I was caught up in this bit of good spirits in the midst of an otherwise gloomy day, wanting to bet on the basic goodness of human nature. *He will help me*, I thought.

Then he leered at me. "It's almost my break," he said. "Come into the back room with me and I'll go over your papers." The crowd pressed against me, and I looked down to avoid tripping over someone's foot. I noticed his scuffed brown shoes were down at the heels. Not the shoes of a savior at all. Worse yet, as I raised my eyes, I saw that his poorly fitting, faded-gray polyester trousers had stains in inappropriate places and an obvious and unprofessional bulge at the crotch.

"Come, come, into the back room with me," he urged. It was about one-hundred degrees in the Rome train station. I hadn't slept in forty-eight hours. I had lost many of my immediate worldly possessions, and the policeman in charge of taking my report concerning my theft was urging me into the back room of the station with him.

I snapped. Suddenly, I was waving my arms and shouting Italian slang I hadn't even been aware I knew: "*Diavolo! Va all'inferno!*" It may or may not have been grammatically correct or made any sense. He stamped my forms.

Finally, my train pulled out of the Rome station. Once again, I was moving south.

This time, it was in daylight. The compartment was breezy but warm, and I was feeling numb from shock, lack of sleep, and the heat. Across from me sat an Italian man, around thirty, handsome, mustachioed—and watching me intently. Speaking Italian, he introduced himself: "I have to travel a lot for my work. We live in Battipaglia." He slid the doors shut and closed the curtains to the aisle. "I've been married just one month. It's difficult being away from my wife so much." I knew he wasn't thinking about thieves.

After a few minutes, he began blowing me little kisses. "*Amore, amore,*" he chanted like a mantra.

A few years before, while eating *cozze con orecchiette* followed by glasses of *grappa* at a friend's house in Rome, my Italian women friends had revealed a secret to me. "Many Italian men," they said, "feel responsible for maintaining the international Italian image of macho virility by attempting to seduce every foreign woman they can. But you know what? Most of them really aren't interested. And many of them aren't such good lovers anyway. They just feel obligated to pretend to seduce. They are counting on you to turn them down."

I looked at the young man across the compartment from me. "*Non, non,*" I said firmly and opened my book. I was on "The Fifth Day" of Boccaccio's *Decameron*. In this section, all the tales were about lovers who achieved happiness after grief or misfortune. A good omen, it seemed. Outside the window, green fields, ancient apartment houses with red shutters, and old women walking with their donkeys flew by. *It's Italy*, I thought. *I'm still alive, and soon I'll be with my friends.* I grinned. In the end, we're just all making our way along as best we can.

My fellow traveler had quietly reopened the curtains and door to the aisle. Like a reprimanded school child, he slid away from me as far as he could on the bench, knees tightly pressed together, and stared into space. Then, glancing at me from the corner of his lovely dark eyes, he noticed my book.

"*Ecco*. Boccaccio. I like very much. Would you like I read to you *un poco*?"

Eagerly, he took my bilingual text and read. The sonorous tones of medieval Italian soothed me as we sailed south into the heart of Italy. Drowsily, I heard him read: "In these tales will be seen the gay and sad adventures of lovers and other happenings both of ancient and modern times."

I closed my eyes and fell into a deep, delicious sleep.

At Home with the Water Buffalo Baronessa

Mozzarella and Ancient Goddesses

I first met Baronessa Cecilia Baratta Bellelli and an entourage of her friends on a misty autumn morning twenty years ago, when I was walking on the beach in Paestum. They came cantering at the edge of the sea on perfectly appointed Thoroughbreds like a mirage out of the mist. I ran down the beach toward them, waving and giving it my best "*Buon giorno.*" They pulled up their gorgeous horses. I explained my admiration for and background with horses and said that I was driving around Italy with my mother and that my interest in ancient goddess archaeology led me to visit the Paestum and the Campana region. Paestum is famous as an ancient center of goddess worship with gorgeous well-preserved temples that were dedicated to Hera and Athena.

Cecilia's shining dark eyes and inviting glance drew me right in.

That day, she invited us to lunch at her family's ancestral estate, and I fell in love with its uniqueness and tranquility, along with the superb food and most of all with Cecilia's warmth and fascinating life. Over the years, I've returned many times to my dear friend Cecilia's *agriturismo* (a working ranch that hosts guests), Tenuto Seliano. Cecilia is a powerful woman in a male-centered land, a suitable modern version of the goddesses who were worshipped here more than twenty-five-hundred years ago.

The Baronessa is on my list of special human beings. Although she comes from generations of Italian aristocratic lineage, standing well over six statuesque feet, she is like a female Zorba. She enjoys both running her ranch and having interesting people around, especially Americans.

For many years, Cecilia was Chairman of the Local Water Board, which oversees the distribution of water to local farmers, a crucial role in this parched agricultural region.

Cecilia affirms: "The water for irrigation in our area is essential for all the farm products. I had money from the government to do important works to save water and give the water to the farmers under sufficient pressure. You are completely right that we women are not appreciated to be in charge of any enterprises. When men have been in charge of the Water Board, they piled up debts and robbed the fund for their own profits. We must say that we women are able to deal like men, but also we are honest."

Less than a five-minute drive from the ranch are the famous Paestum archaeological site and museum. Around 600 BCE, the Greeks founded a city here called Poseidonia in honor of the god of the sea, a sanctuary in honor of the goddess Hera, and a temple to the great goddess Demeter. Ironically, for many years in the past, male archaeologists ignored the thousands of small goddess statues found at the site and described the site as dedicated to male gods. This has now been corrected. In addition to the well-preserved golden Doric temples, excavations continue to unearth Greek treasures. Recently, impressionistic frescoes depicting scenes from everyday life were found. I especially enjoyed a small statute of a goddess who is apparently flexing her biceps. During the cabaret festival in July, one year I watched Nureyev dance by moonlight in and among the temples.

A visit to Tenuta Seliano includes juicy mozzarella at every meal, friendly water buffalo grazing next door, the best-preserved Greek temples in the world where the goddesses of fertility and marriage were worshiped, the lapping Mediterranean a few minutes from your room, and a charming baronessa as our host. Paestum and Tenuta Seliano, a southern Italian resort on a working ranch, dates back to the 16th century on the Italian Mediterranean coast about forty minutes south of newly invigorated Naples. Paestum is famous for its scarlet roses and salmon-colored temples—and is the *mozzarella di bufala* capital of the world. The resort is in the heart of the Campania region of southern Italy. *Campania* comes from the phrase *campania felix*, which means "happy" or "fortunate countryside." The sun is said to shine here two-hundred-thirty days per year.

Vineyards abound, producing excellent local wines, which accompany the superb handcrafted meals. Guests from all over the world share long tables under a shaded grape arbor outdoors or inside in the ancestral dining hall on some mornings and cooler evenings. Breakfast consists of home-baked breads and cake, freshly squeezed orange juice, ripe peaches, and other local fruits, eggs, cereal, and steaming coffee or tea. The ranch produces much of the ingredients for the kitchen, including capers, extra-virgin olive oil, vinegars, limoncello (a lemon liqueur), oranges, figs, strawberry preserves, mushrooms, eggplants, olives, and peppers. Only handmade pasta, pastries, and breads are served, and endless varieties of pizza are baked in the wood-burning oven. Of course, because Campania is the mozzarella capital of the world, delicious fresh mozzarella is enjoyed at most meals, as well as fresh ricotta, another product of water buffalo milk. Frequently, tender homegrown buffalo meat, prepared a variety of ways, is also served, steaming and succulent.

When Cecilia speaks of cooking, her eyes shine and her entire body waves into motion. Lovingly, she explains how each item is selected and prepared, how to know exactly the moment to add it, and the precise blending, heating, and timing. Finally, of course, she reaches into a pan, tastes, and most often serves you something delectable. Her eighty-year-old mother added, "Cooking is one of our most important art forms." Often, Cecilia is invited on cooking tours in the United States to demonstrate Campania regional foods and recipes.

Food preparation is a very special focus at the ranch. Internationally acclaimed chefs, including Alice Waters from Chez Panisse in Berkeley, have visited Cecilia to learn her recipes. Cecilia personally supervises meal preparation. She uses only naturally grown products from the estate. At times throughout the year, the Baronessa offers cooking classes. She specializes in the best of Campania and Neapolitan cooking which, I was interested to learn, includes ancient Greek and Roman influences. Some of Cecilia's special recipes include *Torta Caprese* from Capri, a heavenly almond and chocolate cake; *Pizza Rustica*, a savory ricotta pie, a dark and heady Genovese sauce specially made with hand-selected buffalo meat; and of course, *Insalata Caprese*, fresh mozzarella accompanied by fresh basil, vine-ripened tomatoes, and estate-bottled olive oil.

Nine-hundred doe-eyed, moist-nosed water buffalo, grazing peacefully in irrigated fields on the ranch, provide the fresh milk that is brought daily to Casearia Barlotti, a cheese-making cooperative. The best mozzarella comes from water buffalo, not cow's milk cheese (*fior di latte*), and is preferably consumed within forty-eight hours. It has three times the fat and one-and-a-half times more calcium and protein than cow's milk. At the cheesemaker, the workers heat the milk to just a little over one-hundred degrees Fahrenheit. Industrial producers, especially for export, pasteurize it. "Pasteurizing kills the flavor," says eldest son Ettore. "You can't compare handmade *mozzarella di bufala* with the industrial product. They put the milk in a machine and instantly have mozzarella. We prefer it made by hand." In fact, I learned the name comes from the word *mozzare*, to "break away"; the cheesemakers use their hands to tear cheese off from the larger mass. While visiting the cooperative, I watched the skilled workers form the many sizes and shapes of the finished mozzarella. There were the "little mouthfuls," *cardinalini* or *bocconcini*, which weigh less than two ounces, while a more elaborate braided form is called *trecce*. A woman worker pulled a fresh *bocconcini* out of the foaming milk and popped it into my mouth. The sweet aroma, the delicate flavors on my tongue, and the special squeak truly fresh mozzarella makes against your teeth made me not care what form it was in as I became lost in epicurean heaven.

In addition to the culinary delights offered here, there is much more to a visit to Tenuta Seliano. The fourteen rooms, in addition to a honeymoon suite and one apartment, contain all comforts as well as fascinating antiques from the Bellelli baronage. The stately stone buildings with their red-tiled roofs and decorative wrought iron date from the nineteenth century. A large well-maintained pool is just a few steps across the garden, past some of Paestum's legendary rosebushes and scatterings of Greek and Roman ruins. The Amalfi Coast, Capri, Pompeii, and Herculaneum are all just day trips away.

It is dawn at Tenuta Seliano. Some fluffs of down from my neighbors, the doves, who live in the dove cote on the roof of my nineteenth-century tower room, float by the window. The soft swish-swish sound of irrigation sprinklers wafts in from the surrounding cornfields, which provide meals for the nine-hundred water buffalo. A fresh sea breeze flows through the windows. I think of how this land has provided nurturance and pleasure for so many people for thousands of years and how it will continue to do so. I feel so lucky to be part of this tradition here in *campania felix*—this happy countryside. Cecilia, my Paestum goddess, represents much of Italian culture and history. She is one of my most inspiring models of women's strength and wisdom.

Song of the Sirens

GREEK ISLAND ESCAPADES WITH MY FEISTY MOM

Draw near.... illustrious Odysseus, flower of the Achaean chivalry, and bring your ship to rest that you may hear our voices. No seaman ever sailed his black ship past this place without listening to the sweet voices that flow from our lips, and none that listened has not been delighted and gone on a wiser man.
—Homer, *The Odyssey*

"My darling Aphrodite, I love you. Will you marry me?" The handsome Greek restaurant owner on Santorini pleaded with my eighty-year-old mother as they line-danced to bouzouki music in a late-night bacchanal on a terrace overlooking the Aegean. My mother loved dancing, charming men, and living in general. After being widowed for the second time in her late seventies, she kicked up her heels and, in many ways, relished life to its fullest. During those years, we traveled together frequently and had our own high-spirited odyssey around Greece.

It was twenty years after my first inauspicious voyage there that I returned to the land of Homer, accompanied by my mother, the archetypal Siren. It was natural that we finally shared Athens and the Greek isles together. Greece lived in my imagination from my earliest memories, thanks to her. An avid reader and elementary schoolteacher, she had read Homer's *Iliad* and *Odyssey* and other tales from Greek mythology to me as a child. I imagined sailing the Aegean with Odysseus, visiting the lands of the Lotus Eaters and Circe and the Cyclops for myself. As a college professor, I taught Greek literature. My mother named me Diane, the Roman counterpart of Artemis, the free-spirited huntress. Artemis frolicked in the woods, surrounded by animals, without a thought to marriage or children.

Like my mythological namesake, I enjoyed my adventurous approach to life and my work with animals for many years as a professional horse trainer. Yet, sometimes I thought about what I was missing, having remained child-free. After all, my mother enjoyed having a daughter. I would have no daughter but would continue on my namesake's path. Like Demeter and Persephone, my mother and I were accepting of where our lives had led us.

At our hotel in Delphi, my mother telephoned my room. "Giorgos, our driver, is knocking at my hotel room door. What should I do?" She had been flirting with the poor man for several days as we toured around. How could he know that she was only kidding? "Maybe you should let him in," I advised. "You've been leading him on for days now." Meanwhile holding the phone to my ear in my own room, I was busy with our young tour guide who was licking my cheek and nibbling my shoulder.

A few days later, Mom and I sailed from the mainland at Piraeus to the island of Santorini, this time on the calm seas of early June. The lost Atlantis, first described by Plato, some believe was destroyed in one of largest eruptions in recorded history around thirty-six-hundred years ago to end the Minoan civilization on Crete. Thira, Santorini's ancient name, was reduced to its caldera, now partly filled by the sea and forming a large bay possibly covering the remnants of Atlantis. We stayed in one of the exquisite white cave houses of Oia overlooking the sparkling azure caldera. Touring the island over the next few days, we visited the archaeological excavations underway at Akrotiri, viewing ancient dwellings and roads.

One afternoon, opting for a special experience, I hired a local man with a rowboat to take us to a beach I had heard about. "A nudie beach," I told my mother, who hoped to add yet another act of daring to her repertoire. After a short sail, our boat owner dropped us on the beach, and my frisky mom stripped to her white cotton underpants and bra and enjoyed splashing in the clear warm Aegean. When our oarsman and boat returned after the designated hour or two, he asked us to wade out to the boat. Seeing my mother, still in her underwear, having trouble negotiating the pebbled bottom, he jumped out, waded to shore, and, to her immense delight, scooped her up into his arms, both of them giggling their way back to the rowboat.

One night, we had dinner at an open-air *taverna* with the full moon illuminating the Aegean and the island's chalk-white cliffs. We drank *ouzo* and *retsina*, and ate *souvlaki* and *tzatziki*. "Did you know," a fisherman at our table asked, "that in the old days if a wife was rebellious and refused to have sex with her husband, he would be advised to rub her gently with olive oil for seven days? After that time, she would become sweet and compliant." He winked and passed me the olive oil for my salad. Winking back, I doused my tomato, feta, cucumber, and olives with the ancient golden remedy.

After dinner, musicians on the *bouzouki, karamoudzes, baglama,* and *daouli* drums began to play their irresistible music. Soon, we were all line dancing. One woman said, "We'll teach you an ancient women's dance. This used to be the only dance women were allowed. It was for widows who danced their way off the edge of a cliff." I looked skeptically at the drop at the end of the restaurant terrace. "We won't do that tonight though," they assured me. So, women's rights have made some progress.

I remembered twenty years earlier during the fascist regime when I first visited Greece. Gloria and I got up to dance at a taverna in the Plaka in Athens. We were the only ones on the floor, proudly showing off the steps we had recently learned at our lessons at a San Francisco Greek restaurant. We'd been told that we might have a problem if we danced in Greece. When a handsome man approached us, Gloria said to me, "See, it's okay for us to be dancing." He came so close that I could sniff the ouzo on his breath: "Seet down," he snarled. "Women don't dance in Greece." That same night, Gloria and I did enjoy the plate-bashing party, a banned tradition in those years. The Greek people, inventors of democracy, never really caved in to the fascist regime, always finding ways to rebel. This crazy activity was one of them. Some people at another table invited us to join a birthday celebration. Shades were pulled down on all the windows. "It's against the law these days to break plates," they whispered. Suddenly, everyone jumped up and started dancing and dashing china to the floor until we were crunching broken pottery with every step.

Here on Santorini, although there was no plate-smashing, the chef appeared from the kitchen and began dancing alone in the middle of the floor. We all clapped, urging him to still-higher leaps and slaps of hand on heel. He did several backflips, then tore off one of his sleeves, placing it on his head like a chef's hat. "I hope he doesn't sweat in our tzatziki," said Mom. Seeing her gyrating in her seat, the chef urged her onto the dance floor. He tore off his other sleeve and placed it on her head.

While they were dancing, a new friend joined our table. We'd met a few days earlier in Oia while shopping for traditional Greek gold key-design necklaces. Thanassis and I had flirted and made a tentative date to meet as we left his shop. A charming Adonis of a jeweler, Thanassis, with classic godlike features and the build and olive skin to match, said he often came to this taverna.

After dinner, Mom went back to our hotel overlooking the sea, and I slipped away for a tryst at his apartment where I learned that the Greeks are not only adept at dispensing philosophy. No wonder, I thought, that Lysistrata and her friends wanted their men back in their beds and urged them to return home from endless wars. As the rosy-fingered dawn broke over the white cliffs and blue waters of Santorini, Thanassis drove me back to my hotel, where I caught a few hours of sleep before my mom and I boarded the early-morning ferry to Páros for our next island adventure.

Both my mother and I disliked early mornings, but this one was special as the sun peeked over the blue Aegean and then rose as we sailed into its path. "What a magical trip this is," Mom said. "I'm so lucky to have such a wonderful daughter."

"Ditto, for me," I said. "How many mothers would be the belle of the ball at a Greek taverna and then not mind when I run off with the most handsome Greek on the island?" My mother certainly laid the pattern for me in being open to adventure, joy, and love along life's paths.

Corsica:
My Dinner with Terrorists

EVEN TERRORISTS REACH MIDDLE AGE

What's not to like about a mini-continent containing prehistoric phallic stones, people possibly descended from Neolithic tribes, and towering rocky cliffs that slope to pristine beaches and clear blue seas? A population of poets, dreamers, and political separatists add spice to the mix. For years, I was intrigued by everything I heard about Corsica.

This was the first visit in what became an annual pilgrimage for me.

"Occasional blowing up of French post offices at 3 a.m. at least keeps the McDonald's and Hilton developers away." This was the positive spin offered by French friends in response to the periodic political unrest. On my flight from San Francisco via Nice to Ajaccio, a *New York Times* front-page headline warned, "Machine Gunning of Banks in Corsica Daily Occurrence."

Soon, I was deep among the granite peaks of northern Corsica. My rented Citroën and I wound along back roads in search of the Col de Bavella, the highest mountain pass on the island. It was my birthday, and I intended to spend the night in the mountain village of

Zonza, the nearest dot on my Michelin map to this pass.

After a couple of hours, I saw a sign announcing "Zonza." Twenty or so old stone dwellings in various states of aging were scattered around the small town square. My guidebook promised two small hotels, so I parked my car and began to look around. A few local men were relaxing near a low wall. Behind them, swallows and bats soared over a vertiginous drop. Clear cool high-mountain air and the sweet smell of *maquis*, the ubiquitous Corsican wild herb bushes, seeped into me. Napoleon never forgot his Corsican roots. In chains and blindfolded as he sailed past Corsica en route to prison on the small island of Elba, he reportedly breathed the maquis and knew where he was.

I inhaled and sighed, "Home for the night." The sun exited behind the surrounding incisor-like mountain peaks. It was time to find a place to sleep.

"*Ou est l'auberge?*" I asked a couple of the young locals.

"Down the street." One man pointed off to his right. I drove there but found the hotel door locked and everything dark. A sign read, "Closed tonight to celebrate a family birthday." More aware of my solitude in the deepening dusk, I returned to the square and asked about the other hotel. This time, locals pointed up a steep cobbled road. Back in my car, I floored it and, with a running start, made it up in first gear. At the top was a dark gloomy-looking building with a two-star hotel sign.

A tall, thin man with haunted eyes and a joyful grin bounded toward me in awkward strides, followed closely by two oversized German shepherds. The dogs took turns jumping on the man. "*Arrête. Arrête!*" he shouted at the dogs. One came to a dead stop in front of him, tripping him up. He flew through the air, landing at my feet. Looking up at me, still smiling, he said, with apparent joy, "*Madame, bonsoir. Bienvenue.* You seek lodging?" Unable to stifle my giggles at his Chaplinesque arrival, I asked if he was okay.

"Yes, of course, of course, and I can offer you a choice of rooms," he replied to my inquiry. Inside, he called someone and then fumbled around trying to find the room keys. As he ushered me into one room after another in the cavernous building, it seemed that I was probably the only client that evening. I selected a large room with an enormous four-poster bed and a long balcony that offered a panoramic view of the silent valley and purple mountain peaks.

Relaxing after the long hot drive, I ordered a beer and sat on the balcony, enjoying the tranquility and cool evening air. Swallows swirled around me. I thought about nesting and the feeling of home. My life had followed many trails, but clan and family were not among them. It was my birthday, and no one in the entire world knew where I was. Somehow, being enfolded up there in a crease of those ancient granite peaks gave me a feeling of solitude, yes, but also one of peace and safety. My life has always been an emotional seesaw: the headiness of freedom and solitude balancing against the desire for home and love. Here in Corsica, for some reason, my seesaw was stabilizing. Celebrating my birthday up here felt right.

My reveries on the balcony were interrupted by the loud wails of a baby. Indeed, the hotel was empty except for the room adjacent to the one I had chosen. A young German couple came out onto our shared balcony. They looked harried and tired. "Our baby is teething," apologized the father. My anticipated sound night's sleep in this quiet spot seemed to fade away as I tried to remember where I had stashed my earplugs. But they were friendly people. We toasted each other over another Heineken.

Later when I went down to dinner in a dining room of dark beams and rafters, my gangly host seated me at a table across the room from the German couple. On their table was a small speaker. The owner explained they were wired for sound so that they could hear their baby, whom they left up in the room, if he started to cry. This way they could eat and listen at the same time. We all were entertained with the intermittent cries of their baby. A kind of Muzak for young parents. Here was family life on display.

From the menu, I selected some Corsican specialties: blackbird liver paté, wild boar, and *brocciu*—ewe's milk cheese-filled crêpes—for dessert. How many blackbird livers, I wondered, does it take to produce a slice of paté? My blackbird question remained unanswered, and the boar proved chewy and dry, but the chilled Patrimonio wine was refreshing.

For company, I was reading Dorothy Carrington's book, *The Dream Hunters of Corsica*. This area seemed just the place where the psychic predictors of death that Lady Rose Carrington studied and interviewed would still live and practice their ancient skills. Lady Rose, an English aristocrat, fell in love with Corsica early in her life, moved here, traveled the mountain paths by mule before there were roads, and wrote several excellent books about the island and its culture. In one passage, she describes one of the women she met returning from her mysterious night ritual, bloodied in a trancelike state with her clothes in rags.

At that point, the dining-room door opened, and three Corsicans entered. The men were black-bearded with traditional Corsican rifles under their arms. Apparently, friends of the hotel owner, they all exchanged greetings and sat at the next table. They ordered fresh trout and devoured it whole, holding each small fish by the tail like the raw herring-eaters of the Netherlands.

In between reading, writing in my notebook, and eating, I entertained myself by sneaking glances at the new arrivals and eavesdropping. Dark skin, eyes, and hair: Corsicans are a handsome people who have been battling off one conqueror or another for millennia: Phoenicians and Genoans and most recently the French. Two of the men were probably in their forties, the third one slightly older. One was particularly handsome; he and I caught each other's glances from time to time, lingering slightly longer each time, finally smiling and nodding.

As I glanced over at him, he opened his mouth wide, slipped an entire trout inside, and sucked the flesh off the bones. Then he licked his lips slowly and winked at me.

"*Vous êtes seule?*" he inquired. "You are alone?"

"*Oui, je suis écrivaine américaine.*" ("Yes, I'm an American writer.")

"Ah, Americans don't come here much. They're afraid."

"What do you mean?" I played dumb.

"You know," he pursed his lips at me, "afraid of the *boom, boom*!"

Feigning nonchalance, I asked, "Are you …?"

"*Bien sur.* What brings you to *la Corse*?"

"Well, I've read Dorothy Carrington's books, love the sea, and—" I hesitated, "—am curious about your separatist movement, the struggle for independence from the French. Also, it's my birthday, and I decided to spend it up here on the highest peak in Corsica."

He glanced at the mangled meat on my plate. "You should not be eating boar at this time of year. Although *sanglier*, wild boar, is the dish of the mountains, you are eating meat that has been frozen."

I agreed that my meal was very dry.

He offered me some *aquavit*, a local liqueur made from berries and local fruits. My new companions showed me how to eat trout in one long xylophone riff.

"Come, please join us at our table."

They filled up all our glasses once again. The next glass or two helped to flush away, along with the stringy dried-out boar meat in my throat, any traces of mixed feelings about my clear descent onto the other side of the half-century mark.

My fellow diners were speaking in Corse. For my benefit, they switched back and forth into French. I was curious about their liberation movement and suspected

I was among experts. At this point, we were all getting fairly chummy. "*Alors*," I said, "Can you explain to me about *le FNLC, les séparatistes*?"

"Well, yes. What do you think we've all been doing all these last years?" All three began speaking at once; this quickly turned to shouting and arm-waving. Corsicans are true to their warm Mediterranean genes.

"No, let me; I can explain better!"

"All right. Pascal, you, but don't wander." They addressed the older man who was thin, all elbows and ears, and given to digressions as sinuous as the mountain paths just beyond the door.

"*Oui*, stay on track," one buddy across the table inserted.

"You joke, he can't." Everyone laughed and poured another round of *aquavit*. A lengthy discussion and argument ensued. The French government was to blame. No, it was the Mafia-like Corsican gangs. Hey, we only want to be left alone and live like we always have.

"Well, yes, we plant bombs, but we only do it in banks and post offices when no people are there. How else to keep our island to ourselves?" a younger man interjected.

"I don't follow violence anymore." This man, Ange, had the wonderful angular cheekbones and black beard of old Corsican photos I'd seen. "In fact, I have a tea shop in Bastia. Here's my card. Why don't you come by? It's on your route."

I wondered about the rifles stashed under their table. For centuries, no Corsican went anywhere without a firearm, and apparently, this practice continued in isolated mountain areas—such as where I was spending the night. Ange changed his seat to my side of the table, slid his chair alongside mine, and filled my glass and his again. The others declined.

After a while, one of the others said, "It's time. I have to get home." Suddenly, everyone stood up. Ange and I looked deeply into each other's eyes. I imagined a lovely tryst with a mountain man, a terrorist at that. What a way to get real insights into the Corsican mind and spirit. But then I was tired; there were many windy kilometers to drive tomorrow. He took my hand and kissed my fingertips tenderly and with passion. His black mustache and beard lingered, and his breath caressed the backs of my fingers. "Well, I still have a long drive tonight, and I must open my shop early in the morning," he said. We both shrugged, and he left.

As I nestled into my king-sized, down comforter-covered bed, I chuckled and looked forward to a full night's sleep. Next door, the neighbor baby was quiet for the moment. Yes, I thought, all of us, even terrorists, reach middle age. I looked out at the thousand stars and the full moon over the eerie Corsican mountains and wished myself a happy birthday.

A Neolithic Afternoon

Speed Dating in the Corsican Mountains

The tall man bent his head to fit through the doorway of his goat herder's hut as he greeted me. His eyes were the palest blue with hazel sparks. I shivered as his gaze sizzled into me. I felt that I was in the presence of someone very special. I was in Calasima, the highest and oldest continually inhabited village in Corsica's Niolo region. From my reading as well as information from locals down below in Calacuccia, the main village of this area, I knew that there were still a few people up here who traced their descent from the original Neolithic tribe, the Corsi, who had settled here around 7,000 BCE. In contrast to the shorter, darker inhabitants, these Niolons are blond, blue-eyed, and unusually—over six feet—tall.

The Niolons have been predominantly endogamous, marrying within their group. This has been due both to the suspicious inward nature of the Corsicans as well as the difficulty in finding mates from outside their immediate area since travel has been next to impossible. Until fairly recently, only donkey and mule trails connected these tiny villages high in the granite-peaked mountains to the outside world. Even today, the roads are only wide enough for the smallest car, and if you take too long to blink as you twist along the endless turns, you could easily be sailing off the edge of a cliff. Hence, inbreeding has resulted not only in the blond "giants" but also in an unusually high percentage of demented people.

An immediate example of this was when another man came through a doorway and pressed his unshaven face close to mine. He was gentle, curious, but drooling and clearly not quite normal. His pale eyes peered into mine as he gurgled something in the local Corsican dialect. It was at that point that two friendly women came out the door and pointed out "*la maison du géant*" after I explained that I was an American writer interested in their blond inhabitants.

"He is the giant of the village," one of the women told me as I glanced around the three or four quiet stone-cobbled lanes that composed this tiny hamlet. She had come out of her house partially out of curiosity to see what this stranger was about and partially to rescue me from the first person I met.

"At the end of the street on the left," she said. "That's the man you should meet."

I knocked at the designated door. A handsome wiry man, about six feet tall, his eyes radiated out at me over high chiseled cheekbones. "My name is Saveur Alifonsi." He extended his hand after we had spoken for a few moments. Ever since I had heard the theories about birds as descendants of dinosaurs, I found it fascinating to sit on park benches imagining myself surrounded by little feathered dinosaurs instead of city pigeons. Prehistory, very ancient lineages, and imagining life in the days of the great Earth Mother of those cultures have always intrigued me. Hanging around the dinosaur exhibits in the Natural History Museum in Manhattan was one of my favorite childhood pastimes. Researching the Anatolian Kybele and her predecessor, the earth mother goddess, drew me to the back roads of central Turkey. When I entered the Kybele museum near Ephesus and stood face to face with the eight- to nine-foot statues of the goddess herself, I became "so cold that no fire could ever warm me" (Emily Dickinson's reaction to hearing good poetry). This is how I felt in the presence of Saveur.

"A long time" was all Saveur said when I asked how long his house had been there. Neat blue jeans covered his lean muscular legs. His denim jacket had Mandarin-style toggles instead of buttons or snaps. "*Chinoise,*" he explained. A friend of his who had stopped by across the narrow street to observe my interactions with Saveur lounged against a rocky outcrop in front of one house. He pointed to his own jacket, which was identical to Saveur's. "We bought them together," he shouted. For a moment, I enjoyed the scene of these two buddies on a shopping spree together: male bonding and fashion consciousness high in the Niolo.

"You look like a cowboy," I said to Saveur. He grinned, just a little. "Strong legs to be a *berger*" (shepherd). He slapped his attractive thigh. "Now I'm retired, but for years I followed my goats all over these mountains." He pointed to the jagged granite peaks that surrounded us, which writer Dorothy Carrington described as a monster's open jaws.

"Everyone who comes through here is in twos, always couples. You come alone." He stated this not at all as a come-on or criticism but rather as a bemused observer. The emphasis was on feeling that he and I were quite normal in our singularity, whereas all these others marching about like entrants to Noah's Ark were quite exceptional. I was pleased with his perspective. Traveling around as I do on my own, usually surrounded by couples and families on holiday together, I often feel similarly that my singleness is what makes me different from the rest. Of course, it is best to find one's own situation "normal." There are times when I feel lonely or left out of the world of families and couples, so I strive to remember that my singleness is healthy and positive. Depending on the country and situation, these surrounding couples and families may regard me as a curiosity, a threat, or invisible.

I was feeling such a connection with this man, this Corsi-descended "*géant*," I wanted somehow to tell him. But looking into his calm, bemused eyes, I realized he understood our affinity. These people have lived for so long in such isolated and intimate groups, according to Dorothy Carrington, that they have a highly developed intuitive communication. Words are not necessary. He and I had connected. This feeling of an intuitive or subconscious communication happened to me frequently in the interior of Corsica, *La Corse profonde*.

"Could I find happiness up here with a goat herder?" flashed through my head, which was probably spinning a bit from the thin air. Sometimes I feel like the perennial female Odysseus, always on the quest for new adventure, wisdom, the slightly less imperfect potential mate. This question reoccurs frequently enough throughout my life that I am now able to look at it with almost Zen-like objectivity. I enjoy the immediate experience and know I will, finally, be moving on.

"Do you have any children?" I ask.

"No."

"Have you been married?"

"No."

He looked at me curiously but didn't ask similar questions of me. I thought of the difference in more insistent cultures, like Greek, Egyptian, or Hispanic, where the first question—"Do you have children?"—is a way of finding out if you are married.

"I have no children either," I told him. "I'm divorced. A long time ago."

A most extraordinary interaction then occurred. Giving me one of his soul-piercing looks, Saveur said, "I think we were born the same year." I raised my eyebrows. "1940."

"Um, yes."

"You were born in June as well?"

I nodded. Unbelievable. Here I was ten-thousand miles from San Francisco, and we were comparing astrological signs. And he was guessing correctly.

"Life doesn't change here much." Saveur had moved on to another subject now that we had established some personal connections. While we were talking, a pair of German hikers, a man and a woman, passed through the village without even noticing us standing there or the incredible ancient buildings around them. They were focused on their maps and the road ahead of them. Saveur's eyes twinkled when they met mine. I asked, "If we were here two-hundred years ago, would it have been basically the same as now?"

"Yes, the same."

"What about if you and I could come back two-hundred years in the future?"

"The same, the same. People herd goats, eat, visit, know each other."

Two small boys were riding back and forth on bicycles.

"Of course, sometimes there are disagreements. Everyone participates to settle it." The sense of community, of belonging, was one I envied. In my own life, I have lived most of my years alone, certainly not within a solid community or family such as existed here.

"Before, there were around two-hundred people in the village. Now, only about thirty. Some young people move to Bastia, Marseilles, Paris, to get educated, to find work. Sometimes, they come back. With the *militaire*, I traveled to the Continent and to Black Africa. That was very interesting."

"Did you ever want to leave here, to live anywhere else?"

Without hesitation, he pursed his lips into a kind of frown and shook his head with a definite no. "There are also women here who are tall and blond like me. Most are gone now."

It wasn't clear if he meant dead or moved away, but somehow I sensed that to him the distinction didn't matter.

"Would you like to come inside?" He led me into his small dwelling. A grizzled-looking man was sitting at the kitchen table smoking a cigarette. I had heard a muffled cough from time to time when we were standing outside the doorway. Plates on the table indicated they had just finished lunch. Saveur hastened to clear the table, mumbling an apology to me for the disorder. Actually, his home was immaculate. The kitchen/living room where we were had only the small door to the outside, no window. A fireplace was in one corner. The stone room had the same triangular shape I had seen in all the archaeological sites, both Neolithic and Torrean, I had visited. A hearth sat always at the apex of the triangle. "The fireplace smokes a lot, so I only light it in the winter," said Saveur. He told me wood was plentiful, and water came from one of many "sources." "Some taste better than others," he offered in the way a Californian would discuss their preferred coffee blend or wine.

On one wall atop a table, a television set was neatly covered with a faded but clean old shawl, perhaps his mother's. A black rotary telephone sat beside it. In the opposite corner were a small refrigerator and a gas stove.

Between puffs on his cigarette, the man I came to understand was Saveur's brother coughed occasionally but otherwise said nothing. When I asked to take their photos, the brother cooperatively looked up at me, but

I was not sure how much he understood about what was going on. Saveur lifted his brother's cap. "He was really blond when he was younger." Another case of dementia, I realized.

Saveur was intrigued by the idea that he might appear in a book or newspaper and asked me to send copies of the photos. "You'll come back the next time you come to Corse?" he asked.

"I hope so. I will send photos."

With a clear and firm hand, he wrote his name and address down in my notebook. I wondered if he would write back to me. We shook hands. His handsome face and easy sensuality were framed by his doorway as I left. I thought, *there is a contentment here*. I felt as if I'd just met with a wise old monk or hermit. Clearly, Saveur was an intelligent and witty man. *What must it be like to have spent his life with goats and to live with his demented brother in this tiny village?*

I walked up the hill toward my car. It was parked across from the town cemetery, so I visited the old tombs. The Corsicans are obsessed with death for a variety of reasons. They do not, however, bury bodies in the ground, so impressive crypts dot the landscape wherever you are on the island. And of course, some of them are thousands of years old. In this cemetery, most of the inscriptions dated from the 1940s. Calzarelli and Susini are the most common names. In front of the cemetery was the usual monument to the war dead; more than twenty-thousand Corsicans died in "The Great War." This out of a population of two-hundred-thousand. *Nos enfants morts pour la France* ("Our children dead for France") is an inscription you read all over France as well as in the colonies.

Before I stepped into my car, I looked up at the granite crags. Just below was Saveur's village, and off in the distance appeared another tiny hamlet. Then far below glittered Lake Niolo. Stacked row behind row were the mountains, fading from moss-green to dark-blue to blue-gray and then, beyond view, the sea. I was balanced on a ripple, a crease high on the earth's surface; one step to either side and I would topple off. Yet, I'd just met someone who seemed more calm and solid in his life than most people I know. I carried away with me a little piece of this contentedness as I negotiated the curves on my way down through the ancient mountains of the Niolo.

PART IV
Insights

She pulled in her horizons like a fish-net. . . .
So much of life in its meshes!
She called in her soul to come and see.
—Zora Neale Hurston,
Their Eyes Were Watching God

A Dead Sea Romance

Middle Eastern Conundrums

The gray-haired man with an American accent ordered us to halt and poked his rifle in through the open driver's window near my face.

"Is there something wrong?" I asked.

"There is always something wrong," he replied. "This is Israel."

The year was 1987. My seventy-eight-year-old mother and I were spending the summer traveling in Israel and Greece. The previous winter from her home in Florida, my mother had written to me in Paris, where I was teaching and directing study abroad programs: "Dorothy plans to visit Israel this summer. She invited me to join her and her two children, Joan and Allen. But I'd prefer to travel with you. What if you and I plan a trip and meet them there?"

My mother and Dorothy were best friends; both were widows, my mother a merry one, Dorothy more stolid and fretful. They formed an odd couple, counterpoising each other, my mother's joie de vivre refracting off her friend's concern for every propriety. This balancing act between adventure and security seems to be a coda for many women. From my mother's generation to mine, the fulcrum has shifted. My mother chose a traditional life, married and widowed twice to two dependable, predictable men. Now freed of their constraints upon her, she was kicking up her heels. In my own life, I had begun earlier than my mother to skew toward freedom and adventure. However, that familiar refrain—a desire for the permanence of love and mate wrapped up in one package—chimed in occasionally like an unchained melody.

For my mother, this refrain was always present where I was concerned. Until she saw me properly married off, she felt that she was failing in her Jewish mother role. Dorothy's son was a tenured philosophy professor at a state college in New Jersey—of a suitable age and unmarried. The scheme to push the two of us together during this trip was obvious.

This plan had two major barriers. The first was that Allen and I had once met, albeit briefly, in Florida and were at best neutral toward each other. Allen had long since mummified any spontaneous emotions. These were buried in coils of self-conscious intellectuality just as any connection to the physical universe was smothered under layers of fat. His area of expertise was Aristotle's theories of the natural universe. If any human being was distanced from the natural world—women being a part of the natural world—it was Allen.

The second hurdle for the matchmaking arose as a result of my mother's polyester pantsuits. Perfect in Florida, her bright yellow-pink-and-aqua, drip-dry, wrinkle-proof wardrobe in Israel's sultry climate was like being encased in body-sized plastic baggies. "Be sure to bring cool and light clothing," I had advised her, aware that she was accustomed to an air-conditioned life in Florida.

"I can't understand it," she huffed and puffed at me. "I wear these things all the time in Florida." The mother-daughter relationship is based on a negotiation between love and exasperation. So off we went in search of cool cotton dresses for Mom.

Entering into the shadowy, convoluted, narrow streets of Jerusalem's Old City, we drifted from alley to alley. Surrounding us were tiny stone booths, each dimly lit interior offering piles of oranges and vegetables in hues from palest yellow to deepest green, round and gourd-shaped, some recognizable, some not. Rainbows of brightly colored silk scarves hanging from beams swayed above our heads. Some stands offered jewelry, intricately designed silver pieces set with the turquoise-like Eilat stone, which is mined only in Israel. Some of the tiny streets were dark, and a cool dampness flowed over our perspiring faces; turn a corner and stultifying heat and sunlight rained down on our bodies. Sometimes, enormous white canopies floated over our heads, hung there to screen out the brilliant sunshine. In some quarters, intriguing smells entered our nostrils from pans and pots sizzling and boiling with local foods. Varieties of spices lined some streets, their musk-like, peppery, or piquant aromas filtering into our nostrils.

Never far from sight slouched the omnipresent Israeli

soldiers, always armed and waving their weapons about or resting them on their knees while they joked with each other and sometimes at passersby. Recognizing us as Americans—my mother's short curly white hair and sensible American walking shoes were giveaways—occasionally the soldiers would show off a few words of English. "Hello, where are you from?" Or if my mother were looking in the other direction, they would lick their lips suggestively and flash me a flirtatious glance.

Still not a cool summer dress in sight. "I've had enough. Let's go back to the hotel. How will we find our way back? I want a taxi," complained Mom. Frankly, I wasn't sure what the shortest route would be to get out of the labyrinth that had engulfed us. We were now wandering in the Muslim section. A few minutes before, I'd peered through an ancient gate and could see the Temple Mount and Dome of the Rock.

"Maybe we should go wail at the Wailing Wall," I suggested to my mother.

"Thanks a lot."

"Would you like to sit down and have a rest and a cup of tea?" inquired a tall, dark, angular, approximately thirty-year-old Palestinian who was standing in front of a stone storefront. His large hazel eyes were soft and twinkling, offering at once comfort and a hint of other possibilities. He wore a Western-style, black- and red-checkered shirt, sufficiently unbuttoned to display a lushly hairy chest that made my fingers twitch with desire to run themselves through its promise. Miraculously, behind this young man hung a neat display of soft cotton dresses as well as skirts and blouses. My mother and I both heaved deep sighs, looked at each other, and chorused, "Yes."

And that's how my mother and I met Mohammed, who became another barrier to parental matchmaking activities. The following day and days, Mohammed left his clothing shop in the Old City in the charge of a friend, Ghassan, and accompanied us on our sightseeing adventures. By the end of the third day, Mohammed was calling my mother "maather" in his accented English. She loved it and him, but a Palestinian son-in-law had never been part of her plans for me. By the time Allen and his family arrived, Mohammed and I had already spent a happy week together.

The afternoon after Mohammed and I were stopped at the entrance to the Hebrew University, he and I returned to the hotel where my mother and I were sharing a room. She and her friends were out shopping and then planned to go out to dinner. This was to be the first time Mohammed and I would have time alone in a room with a bed. Like most unmarried Palestinian men, he lived with his large extended family. I had visited them at home, and they were very hospitable, even leaving us alone together in the living room. But always his mother, aunt, and several sisters were just on the other side of the drapery, which served in lieu of a solid door.

Hence, most of our lovemaking had taken place within the confines of my tiny rental car. It had been tender and, of necessity, imaginative. Mohammed was sixteen years younger than I. I was only the second woman with whom he had made love. His apprenticeship state along with his height—well over six feet—made for challenging coupling sprawled across the back seat of the car with legs extending into the front seat. He wanted more than anything to please me, and certainly his physical attributes along with his passion made up very well for what he lacked in experience. Also, I delighted in the sites of our lovemaking: beside the Wall of Jericho, at the gates of the Church of the Holy Sepulchre, atop the Mount of Olives at sunset. In my guidebook, I read about a church called Our Lady of the Spasm and very much wanted to make love there. Unfortunately, it was within the walls of the Old City and proved to be perpetually circled with crowds.

Back in my hotel room, Mohammed was quietly reading a newspaper and waiting for me to shower. The bathroom was warm and steamy, so I had left the door wide open. Mohammed was very modest. Sharing a shower was not part of his repertoire. In his family's home, as in most Arab homes, showers were cold and outside the main part of the house in a separate and usually austere building.

Just as I stood drying myself in front of the bathroom mirror, the door to the hotel room opened, and in waddled Allen. Stunned, he stared at me, said "Hello" to Mohammed, and, backing out, twisted the key so hard in the lock that it broke off in his hand.

"Look at that—the key's broken off," he observed in his objective Aristotelian manner.

Wrapping a towel around myself, I asked, "What are you doing here?"

"Your mother gave me the key to the room. I didn't like the restaurant they had chosen for dinner, so she said I could wait here."

I was furious with my mother's deliberate intrusion on my privacy. No doubt, she imagined I might be here with Mohammed and, in her stealthy way, sent Allen up to somehow stir himself into the soup. Well, he certainly had. But he needed to be strained out of it.

Allen remained at the wide-open door, waving half of the key at me and Mohammed. "They should use better quality keys," he asserted. Our plans for slow, luxurious lovemaking were clearly shelved for the time being.

"Someone call the desk to ask them to send up a repair person," I snapped, continuing to dry myself behind the now-closed bathroom door, where it was stifling.

"Have you studied Muhammad's life?" I heard Allen ask. Mohammed continued reading his Arabic newspaper and shrugged as though the question held no meaning for him. We were all awaiting hotel personnel to rescue the broken key from the lock so that we could leave for dinner. Still in the bathroom, I was now mostly dressed and combing my hair, applying eye makeup, and putting on jewelry.

"What do you mean?" Mohammed asked, looking up calmly from his newspaper. I couldn't tell if he was taunting Allen or was genuinely interested in Allen's question and opinions. I realized, even if Mohammed didn't, that Allen was baiting him. In this culture, Muhammad is part of people's everyday lives, not something they give lectures on. Allen was trying to impress me with his intellectual superiority to Mohammed.

"Muhammad and the Quran are part of our culture. We grow up knowing about them."

Finally one, two, and eventually a crowd of hotel workers arrived. They scratched their heads and laughed back and forth, swapping what I was sure were very funny comments in Arabic. Mohammed looked amused as well. "We've never seen anything like this before," they told me in English, "a key broken off in the lock." Into my head popped thoughts of the Jewish ritual where the bridegroom stomps on a glass and breaks it at the end of the wedding ceremony. Well, this breakage was as close as Allen would get to stomping on my glass. We left Allen in the room with the hotel staff tending to the broken lock and went to dinner. "See you in the morning," Allen reminded me.

As part of our ongoing travels around Israel, my mother and Dorothy, along with daughter Joan and son Allen, were planning to drive to the Dead Sea and stay for two nights in a kibbutz hotel located near the Sea and Masada. Built by King Herod in the last century BCE, Masada is the most significant archaeological site in Israel. A UNESCO World Heritage Site and ancient stone fortress located high above the Dead Sea, it was the site of Jewish resistance to Roman armies.

I looked forward to visiting this special place and also the opportunity to have more time with Mohammed, who was eager to join us on this adventure. My mother and I were happy to have him with us. We agreed that Mohammed would stay with me in one room with Mom in a separate room. While she understood that he and I were enjoying each other's company, she also knew my penchant for falling in love—temporarily.

"I'm just worried about Mohammed," she said. "I'm afraid he's going to be hurt when you leave." I was enjoying this budding relationship, not thinking much about where it might lead. My own desire for love and intimacy followed a similarly cautious pattern: testing the waters with one or two toes but making sure no major waves soaked me entirely. My mother always seemed to deny any vulnerability on my part.

Our Masada adventure was about to become more complicated. Two days earlier, Dorothy, son Allen, and daughter Joan had accompanied us into the souk, saying, "We want to see your Palestinian friend's store." They'd been amused at what passed for a store in the Old City. "Bloomingdale's it's not," Joan was quick to say. Joan was somewhat stylish in a chain-store way. Totally submissive to her mother, Joan had a tightness around her mouth and eyes, and apparently spent too much time with her mother. She looked like she needed a good frolic. While we were all at the shop, we met Ghassan, Mohammed's close friend and business partner, a pleasant and handsome young man. Ghassan and Joan seemed to be attracted to each other, Joan clearly flirting with him.

In the morning when we picked up Mohammed at his house, he surprised us with the news: "Joan has invited Ghassan to join us." I hadn't expected this but thought it sounded like a fun idea. Perhaps Joan was planning a romp beside the Dead Sea with Mohammed's attractive friend. I assumed that Dorothy and Joan had worked out the sleeping arrangements, reserving adequate rooms at the kibbutz hotel.

The trip from Jerusalem to the Dead Sea took a few hours. We drove in two cars, passing Jericho, steaming in its humidity at 800 feet below sea level. A few miles southeast of Jericho, the Dead Sea came into view. Just across the wide blue expanse of water, the Jordanian border was visible. At the Kibbutz Guest House, Ein David, located on the shore of the Dead Sea and adjacent to the Masada archaeology site, my mother, Mohammed, and I checked into our rooms. The hotel consisted of small guest houses scattered on the hillside just above the sea.

The plan was for everyone to meet in the cafeteria-style restaurant for dinner. I noticed a crowd gathering out by the swimming pool. "It's a wedding," a kibbutznik told me. "You are welcome to join us." The residents seemed to tolerate us as necessary to their kibbutz's survival but remained closed and somewhat haughty. However, their sneers and rejection of Mohammed were obvious. My mother and I decided to take a look at the wedding.

Mohammed refused and said, "I'm going to take a walk." He seemed sad. He spoke perfect Hebrew, although with an accent. In Jerusalem, he had told me proudly how he had both Jewish and Palestinian friends. "We're all brothers," he said, even introducing me to some Israeli soldiers who called him by name. I had thought that people like Mohammed were the future of Israel. However, here I saw the hostility with which the Jewish settlers treated him simply because he was Palestinian. The accent and his appearance apparently were the key to instant rejection by almost all the Israelis we met on our travels. I realized that up until now we had spent much of our time either alone or in Palestinian areas.

After dinner, Mohammed and I slipped away to the fully moonlit banks of the Dead Sea. It was my first close-up view of this strange ancient body of water. The full moon lit up the shoreline and glittered on the water. We sat at a small table outside a café where a Greek Israeli musician was performing. The music reminded me of Greece but with a Middle Eastern flair. The tones—poignant and romantic but also tragic—seemed to combine the ethos and passion of the two cultures.

Full moon over Masada, I thought. Mohammed and I looked into each other's eyes. I was enjoying the feeling of falling in love. For Mohammed, this was real. For me, it was real in the moment, but I had lots of other lives far from this desert, these old walls, this dead sea. At the moment, he was young, optimistic, and idealistic. He seemed to have climbed out of his sorrow. "Everyone is my friend," he reiterated, trying to deny the rejection he had experienced "We all get along—Palestinian and Jew. We are all brothers."

"What about the young people in the kibbutz this afternoon? They treated you so rudely."

"Oh, some people are unpleasant. Is that not true

in America, in France? But generally, everyone can be kind to each other." I wondered if he was being naïve or if such generosity of spirit would finally settle an ancient dispute.

All over the Middle East, any public display of affection is unacceptable. That night on the way back to the hotel, we sneaked a few hand squeezes and a stroking of a back here and there. Now and then on an isolated path, we attempted a purloined kiss. "No, no, we must be careful," Mohammed said.

We returned to the kibbutz, where a war was brewing. It had nothing to do with Middle Eastern politics. Dorothy and Joan were standing in front of our room, obviously in a snit. "What are you going to do about Ghassan?" they asked me. "He can't sleep outside. He might get shot." They had seen the Israeli soldiers patrolling everywhere.

"What do you mean? Isn't he staying with you, Joan?"

"I wouldn't do that to my mother. He and Mohammed should stay in this room, and you sleep with your mother." Allen had his own room.

"Well, if he can't stay with you, why not have him share Allen's room?"

"Allen's already asleep. We wouldn't wake him," Dorothy piped up.

By now, I was totally exasperated. I said goodnight, pulled Mohammed in with me, and closed our door. Mohammed and I crawled into bed. I felt happy to be with him and wondered if I should feel guilty. We hugged and kissed—a little. Either Mohammed's reticence, inexperience in kissing, or a response to cultural taboos hampered our spontaneity. Fortunately, his youthful impetuousness managed to put aside these taboos as we both enjoyed the feeling of budding love. Still, he didn't take an active role except in the most basic ways. I guided him into me, then asked him to roll onto his back so that I could satisfy myself by rocking on top of him. Like him, his penis had a youthful exuberance that was both sweet and exciting. I squeezed him hard and we both fell through wave after wave, finally reaching a calm sea far offshore. He was pleased and relieved to have satisfied me.

At breakfast the next morning, we learned that unfortunate Ghassan had slept on the floor in Dorothy and Joan's room. Dorothy and Joan refused to speak to me or Mohammed. Somehow they had managed to forget that Joan had invited him on this excursion. They blamed everything on me.

We went down to the sea. The waters of the Dead Sea are thick and brownish, containing thirty-percent solid matter. Moving in its waters is almost impossible. It is like trying to swim or roll around in a rapidly solidifying cake mix. Twist as you will, your body remains in its original position. The dense water seemed an appropriate metaphor for Middle Eastern politics as well as Western prejudices, mired as they are in a congealed set of assumptions and beliefs. Likewise, it was emblematic of my own ambiguity about my romantic life. If finally I chose to remain with one man, would that be comforting and supportive like the Dead Sea? Or would I become alarmed and flounder in vain to change my course—because I was stuck?

One month after leaving Israel and returning to San Francisco, Mohammed sent me a formal proposal of marriage. "Someday you will need a man to take care of you, and I want to be that man," he wrote. I was touched and pleased, but my main emotion was fear. I was afraid that this man wouldn't go away; afraid of my longings for permanence and love; afraid to hurt him; afraid that our class, education, and cultural differences were too great; afraid that what he really wanted was his green card and didn't really love me. Or perhaps he loved the idea of me but couldn't possibly know who I really was.

I wrote him a kindly worded letter of refusal.

We stayed in touch, each writing one letter a year. Then, ten years later, I received a phone call. "It's Mohammed. I am coming to the States to visit my brother, who is living in North Carolina. I would like also to come see you in San Francisco. I am looking forward to being with you again." I was excited but worried.

"What are your plans? When will you be going back?"

"We shall see. Maybe I will stay in the States. Maybe I will marry. We'll talk about it when I visit you."

"One week. You can stay one week." I decided it would be good to set clear parameters.

I met him at the airport and drove him to my house. I was confused about whether we would sleep together or if it would be more prudent to have him stay in the guest room. Mohammed was now forty years old; he had filled out but was still handsome and thoughtful. He had a more guarded look about him. On one cheek was a long scar. "A rock hit me one day while I was driving my bus." That had been his job for several years after his shop was forced to close. Palestinian rock-throwers had struck him in the face. He could have been killed many times. He was just five minutes behind the bus that was blown up the previous year. "It's very different here in the States, the way all kinds of people—Christians, Jews, Muslims walk near each other without the hatred and anger and fear we see all the time in Israel. It's very nice here," he said.

Permanently paired people often view the serial lovers of single people as somehow less correct than being with the same person through the years. They seem to feel that if you kept yourself purely alone, an appropriate mate would materialize. What they don't realize is that while you are waiting, life would be passing you by. Is a patchwork of intimate moments somehow completely inferior to one long and continuing connection? No doubt, compatible mating is terrific. But certainly within even a good long-term relationship, some moments are better than others. Because they are with the same person, does that make those moments superior? Patchwork quilts can be lovely and more interesting than one solid blanket.

I decided it would be intriguing to share a week of love and intimacy with Mohammed. After showing him around my house, I said, "Come stay with me in my room."

"No," he replied, "It's different now. I'm older. I won't have sex unless it is with my wife. I'll stay in the guest room." He really meant it. Muslims, Middle Eastern guys, don't fool around. When they make love and take a wife, that's it for life. There is something really endearing about the whole approach. But then I've always preferred the chase to a possible Thomas Hardy aftermath and a less-than-idyllic life after the wedding.

One evening during a fireside dinner while Mohammed was staying with me, I thought, *What if I had said yes to him ten years ago? Would we be happily married now in Jerusalem, with babies, and me at the university surrounded by an adoring husband and all of his family?*

Now that was an ending a more traditional woman—say, Dorothy or perhaps even my mother—could have been happy with. But not me, not me.

I wrote Mohammed after he returned to Israel:
I hope we can stay very good friends, and perhaps someday if I am ever back in Israel, we will see each other. Take care of yourself, and be careful. My mother too said to me that she was thinking about you often as she hears the bad news from Israel and hopes you are safe.

Dancing on the Wine-Dark Sea

Audrey's Final Dance

Five years later, I returned to Greece, this time accompanied by my mother's ashes. My plan was to sprinkle them in the waters off Santorini, a place where we had both had such fun together. I lay awake in my hotel in Athens, thinking about my mother's recent death. I was in the same hotel, not far from the Plaka with a view of the Acropolis, where my mother and I stayed as we began that last madcap voyage together. I thought about my mother reading Greek myths to me at my bedside many years ago. Now I was returning to Greece to scatter her ashes in Homer's "wine-dark sea."

So many memories here. Greece, ancient and modern, had intertwined itself through my life. My mother's death marked the end of my family. Yes, I was alone, but my life was a satisfying one—and there were lots of adventures still to come.

Suddenly, my bed began to jump around the room. The hotel rocked, and when I looked out the window, it seemed that the Acropolis itself was undulating. I braced myself in a doorframe for stability as I learned to do over the years living in California. In an unfamiliar place far from home, I could only hope for the shaking to stop. I learned later that a major earthquake had jolted Greece. The epicenter was near Sparta. Hotels had fallen and hundreds of people had been killed although Athens, where I was at the moment, and the immediate surrounding areas were largely unaffected.

Just like my own life's transitions at the moment, the quake reminded me of the fragility of everything, including the ground on which we stand, which really is a crust of land floating on fire and water.

I ventured out of my hotel and wandered the familiar streets around the Acropolis and the Plaka, the most ancient area of Athens, where I had spent happy times with my mom in the past. This city and country with so much history and continuing culture and living myths always seem to ground me, even in the time of earthquakes, which have occurred here for millennia.

After a few days in Athens, I took a ferry from the nearby port of Piraeus over to Santorini, where I had arranged to meet some friends for a women's creativity retreat. Because my mother had loved her time in Greece and flirted shamelessly with every handsome young Greek who crossed her path, I felt she'd like being out there in that clear blue water where new generations of young Greeks would be frolicking. As we sprinkled her ashes, some friends and I chanted a poem I had written for the occasion:

HYMN TO MY MOTHER, TO AUDREY

Summer 1995—My friends and I chanted this hymn as we sprinkled my mother's ashes on San Francisco Bay; the Aegean off Santorini, Greece; the Seine in Paris; and the Atlantic in New Jersey and West Palm Beach, Florida.

To my mother, to Audrey, to our friend:

As your mother, Anna, and her mother, Esther,

And thousands of women for thousands of years,

I release your ashes and your bones
And guide your spirit back to the seas

The seas that circle and surround

Where you adventured and loved and laughed for
 eighty-five years of life.

You gave me life:
I release your life back to the sea.

You gave me love:
With love I see you off
on the winds and the waves.

You gave me strength and courage:
I release the strength of your bones and
the courage of your ashes
   to the seas.

You taught me about joy and adventure:
I honor your joyfulness and adventurousness

In the waves and the winds and the sand.

You danced music into my life:
I send you dancing on all the seas and beaches of the world.

You gave me peace.

I wish you peace with the winds and the waves and the seas,

which are always and everywhere.

—Diane LeBow

As I loosed Mom's ashes into the azure water, the calm bay suddenly sizzled and glittered with the sparkles of a million diamonds. "Wow, what is happening?" one of my companions gasped. This was the stuff of Greek myths, and we looked at each other wide-eyed. Very possibly by now, my mother was playing the coquette with Charon as he ferried her across the Styx, or was enticing Hades himself into a line dance.

Love on the Line

COURTSHIP BEFORE CELL PHONES

I travel a lot, and mostly I travel alone. When I enter a public phone booth to check in with friends back home, sometimes I feel like I'm opening a mystery novel. I never know what news awaits me, and more than once, love has rung its way into my life—or disconnected from it—in these places.

"I hate to tell you this way, but your visit to stay with me in Hawaii just won't work out now," his voice said on my answering machine. It was at least one-hundred degrees. Familiar symptoms followed: crazy heart rate, a wash of sweat over my body. I did a quick survey of my life—past, present, and future—and found it sadly wanting.

I was high in the Corsican mountains, exploring the fourteen-hundred BCE Bronze Age archaeological site of Pianu di Levie, and had decided to stop in the sole phone booth to access my messages back in California. After two months in France and Corsica, I was to be heading home in five days and then on to a remote area in Hawaii to spend a few weeks with my lover of the last six months, a man I had known for the past three years. I'd been looking forward to this visit, to the love and coziness, to being cared for, after what had been a rigorous and lonely two months. I stood in the phone booth with my tickets, reservations, and dreams and wondered what to do.

My booth was in the sun, surrounded by the village's barren and dusty tiny plaza. In order not to suffocate, I held the folding door of the booth open with one hip. I called my 88-year-old writer friend, Dorothy Carrington. These days, I seemed to be collecting a certain kind of role model: older women writers all over the world, living well and creatively on their own. Dorothy tops my list.

During the next few days, I had been planning to visit her at her home in Ajaccio, Corsica's largest town and Napoleon's birthplace. Without pausing for a breath after hearing my romantic woes, she said: "That's not at all surprising. Men are hunters. Only one in four is at all capable of making any kind of emotional commitment. And in any case, you wouldn't want a man around all the time anyway."

"What about sex?"

"Ah, well, yes. That is a problem. When I turned seventy, my desire for sex just walked out the door, and I've been much more at peace ever since. So, are we going to get together?"

"What about lunch?"

"That's too much. What I really want is a banana split." This stated with an English aristocratic "baa-nahna." I was already beginning to cheer up.

The next day, I found myself on the white-sand beach near the fishing village of Campomoro, looking out at southwest Corsica's translucent turquoise sea. The blank sentinel eyes of a fourteenth-century Genoese watchtower oversee this area of the Gulf of Valinco. A voice interrupted my solitude: "You seem to be quite *triste*; perhaps I can cheer you up." I looked up. The voice was attached to a tall, olive-skinned, hazel-eyed young Corsican. "My name is Christian. May I bring my towel over here?"

As I explained my situation to him, he came to a rapid conclusion. "You must stay on here for two more weeks. There's a phone booth just above by the cafe. I'll help you call the airlines and we'll change your flights. In fact, I'm not even using my apartment these weeks; please feel free to stay there."

I awoke the next day to birds' songs. Below me, the sea was blue and calm. The nightmare had passed. The wrenching of flesh from flesh. On another isle, ten-thousand miles to the west and twelve hours earlier in time, the volcanoes still bubbled and smoked and exploded. He slept, perhaps dreaming guilty dreams of me. Here the volcanoes were calm, mature, covered with green maquis, smoothed by the centuries. But still, the form of the volcano remained. The potential was there, of passion, eruption. The bells of Propriano sounded in the distance, below in the town. My new lover arrived, bearing fresh warm croissants.

"How many lovers have you had?" he asked me.
"I don't know."

"More than me, I'll bet."

Little does he know, I thought.

"Maybe finally you are meeting the right one." He was charming and convincing and a wonderful antidote. My injection theory of recovering from a broken heart worked once again: Make love with another man, and like swallowing an antihistamine pill, you begin to recover. Replacement juices and hormones do their job.

My Corsican adventure was not the first time a rendezvous in a phone booth had sent me reeling. My attraction to and fear of phone booths began years ago. In 1961, I was a senior at a women's college on the East Coast and living in dormitory housing. There was a single phone booth for about thirty women. When a call came in from a man, whoever answered the phone would shout up to your room, "A phone call." If it was a woman's voice on the line, they would say, "A call."

One evening, the promising words "phone call" summoned me to the phone. I had been dating an Irish Catholic man, Kerry Keegan, who attended an Ivy League men's college in New England. I was in love with Kerry—and I was going through a pregnancy scare. A few days earlier, I had called him to tell him that my period was late. My hope was that he was calling me. Instead, a strange male voice identified itself: "This is Father Fitzpatrick. Kerry has shared your news with me. I am sure a smart college girl like yourself will know how to take care of this problem and not upset a fine family like the Keegans." Clearly, my Jewishness had placed me somewhere in the category of an untouchable in those intense anti-Semitic days. The phone booth was suddenly stifling as I hung up and dragged myself back to my room.

Other times, phone booths yielded happy surprises. When Abdallah Sidi called me in Paris from Tunis to say "*Je t'aime*," I had expected neither his call nor the message but was very pleased. We had met just a few weeks before when I had spent ten days at a Tunisian coastal resort. During gray rainy Parisian winters when the sun becomes an atavistic memory, Tunisia is an inexpensive and sunny getaway for the French.

There in Tunisia, at a Club Med-style resort near Hammamet, a creative maître d' had seated me at the same table with probably the only single man in the dining room. Abdallah, an economist with the Tunisian government, was staying at the hotel while conducting government business in the nearby villages. He spoke French well but with a Tunisian accent. His English was another story. He used wonderful literal translations from Tunisian like "I have the nose" to explain that he was getting a cold and had congested sinuses. We talked during meals, met for after-dinner coffee, became friends, and finally something more.

Americans take phone booths for granted. In Tunis, the only public phones are in the crowded post office. Waiting in line to call can sometimes take an hour. Then, at least in the days when I knew Abdallah Sidi, you were limited to three minutes per call. So when he phoned me in Paris, recalling the crowds and the heat in that area of Tunis, I appreciated what he was going through. I pictured the old souk, the marketplace, just behind the post office, the same souk where French friends and I had gotten trapped during a flash flood and had to pay a local boy to lead us out, floodwater up to my knees, clutching over my head the maroon-and-gold woven dress I had just purchased.

"I want you to come spend the summer with me in Tunis," he said. "Friends have made an apartment available. There won't be any furniture, but that's not a big problem." I thought about sleeping on the floor in a non-air-conditioned apartment in summertime Tunis. Abdallah was a very nice man—intelligent, handsome, divorced, and intense. He had introduced me to what seemed a rather kinky aspect of Muslim lovemaking: silence. "You must make no sound because Allah can hear. When you are satisfied, you may say, 'Okay.' But only that." At the time, I didn't wonder about the illogic: Couldn't Allah see as well as hear? Back in Paris, I had been thinking about Abdallah a lot and missing him.

"I want us to be married. We have to speak quickly because my three minutes are almost up." My mind whirled. "Click, click, buzz" went the dial tone as we were cut off. As I hung up, I sighed a small "thank you" to the Tunisian phone system and began planning my letter of adieu.

Sometimes, phone booths aren't for phone calls. I discovered this while taking a cruise with my mother. She was a traveler; in her last years and in failing health, she found cruises a means to keep up her wanderings. As claustrophobic and sedate as I found them, I accompanied her on several. One was unmercifully long: three weeks from the Caribbean through the Panama Canal and up to San Francisco. A man who sat at the next table from us and I eyed each other, spoke, danced, and finally tried to find a private place. He was sharing his cabin with his young son, and I was sharing mine with my mother. After midnight, wandering around the ship, we discovered an odd room off the gambling casino that, strangely enough, had a phone booth in it. The room appeared to be deserted, so we started to hug and kiss. Eventually, I ended up on the little seat in the phone booth. Enjoying ourselves immensely, we burst out laughing when a member of the crew started to enter the room, saw us, and grew wide-eyed. "Is everything all right here?" he asked.

And now I sat by the Gulf of Valinco, thinking about loves that ended and began in public phone booths. I'm all right now, I thought, after reflecting on my current situation. Laurel blossoms fell on me from the surrounding trees. My head had cleared; Corsican seas are soothing, blue, and full of wonder. I was on Prospero's island—and there wasn't a phone booth around for miles.

The Flotsam and Jetsam of Love

RE-COLLECTIONS OF A SINGLE WOMAN

Most people who have been single for as long as I have look back at their patchwork of relationships: the joys, the eccentricities of partners, the heartaches of endings. In addition to these memories, for me, there is something else.

I look around me and see kitchen utensils. The men in my life, for various reasons—pretty obvious ones actually—have showered me with culinary and other kitchen-oriented tools. So, even though our days of passion have passed, not only am I not left with a broken heart but I am also not left empty-handed. Instead, my kitchen drawers and cabinets overflow with their offerings.

It is not as though I am unable to cook. In fact, I was married for nine years to a man who refused to touch paring knife or pot—but that's another story. I did churn out the necessary meals during that period, albeit often grumpily. Since my single days commenced more than twenty-five years ago, I have actually owned houses with kitchens. I do eat on a regular basis; I've even been known to host dinner parties for my friends. Many of my wedding shower gifts, now decades old, still languish in my kitchen drawers: a potato masher, steam iron, poultry shears, egg beater. Some of these items I use—occasionally.

My passions are many: literature, music, art, horses, politics, travel. I enjoy fine cuisine and dining *à l'américaine* as well as abroad. I eat well and healthfully. But food preparation is not high on my list of life's pleasures. Post-feministly, over the past twenty-five years or so, men seem to have dived into the culinary arts with great gusto. I sometimes wonder if my ex-spouse is part of this crowd, although I highly doubt it.

Happily, into my life have meandered men who love to cook. I bless them and wish for them to flourish and multiply. I am sure they have gone on to prepare many a romantic repast for other grateful single women.

One atavistic male tendency, no doubt residue of millennia as hunters, is clearly seen in the male insistence on quality knives that are properly sharpened. "What this house really needs is a professional French chef's knife," said Mark, my first serious partner after my divorce. When I met Mark, he was dedicated to honing his artistry in French cuisine. By the end of our romantic connection, he had done an amazing flipflop over to macrobiotics—which, for me, made our parting a good deal more palatable. Mark was a grant writer and nonprofit consultant, a kind, intelligent, and serious man. He was dedicatedly pro-feminist. This was an enormous asset during the heady feminist revolutionary days of the early-seventies. I would stagger home after a hard day fighting the dragons of sexism and patriarchy, and he would chop, peel, and sauté, finally setting a delicately seasoned *gigot d'agneau* with *haricots verts, riz,* and a nicely chilled Sancerre before me.

But Mark riffled through my jumbled drawers and cabinets and found a serious void. The holiday season was upon us, and gifts appeared. Under my Christmas tree, no baubles nor bangles but instead, beautifully wrapped in purple-and-green-striped paper with a large bow, was a serious, hefty, black-handled, steel Sabatier chef's knife with its sloping triangular blade that sliced effortlessly through beef for bourguignon, shallots for sautés, and anything else that appeared on the wooden cutting board. As gentle a man as Mark was, his gift proved more than I could handle.

"I shall prepare our dinner tonight," said I on New Year's Eve. "For once, you can just sit back and relax." Chopping and slicing away, relishing the power of my new tool but lacking the craft, suddenly the tip of the little finger of my left hand became part of the salad ingredients. Red blood streaming, clutching the flapping fingertip, I shuffled out to the car and off we rushed for a late-night visit to the Stanford Medical Center emergency room. Fortunately, little fingers' tips grow back on very nicely.

In contrast to kind and considerate Mark, at least one of my lovers was far less gentle than his gifts. Each morning, I brew my tea in a cozy little brown handcrafted teapot. While sipping my English Breakfast brew, if I raise my eyes, atop one cabinet is a globe of the world. While these two items may not seem to be related, in fact, they were given to me by Antonio, a womanizing, globe-trotting jock who also loved theater and concerts and hosting our friends for banquet-level meals. His specialty was an entire meal of abalone that, as a scuba diving instructor, he collected in the chilly waters off the northern California coast. Once, we had fifteen people around the table, which involves quite a lot of abalone. We had abalone soup, abalone ceviche, and grilled abalone steaks.

That summer, Antonio was teaching at the college where he was a physical education instructor. The Berlin Wall had just come down, and I was invited to join a group of disgruntled American socialist journalists for a month of interviews and exploration. Because Antonio couldn't get away, we agreed that I should go. After all, a month is not so long.

Antonio's domesticity, expressed by his offerings such as my teapot and his playing host to my friends—and his avidity for world travel—was reflected in his gift of my globe. These were marvelous attributes, and so was his skilled, passionate lovemaking. Unfortunately, he liked to share the latter with as many willing recipients as possible. So, when I called him from a phone booth in JFK Airport to joyfully say that I would be home in a few hours to continue our connection of the past seven months, I was stunned when he gave me some startling news. "Oh, everything will be different now. I've gotten back together with Darlene; she's someone I was with a few years ago. I'll still pick you up at the airport though if you want."

Antonio is long gone, but my little teapot and globe continue to serve me well.

Some of my lovers' contributions to my connection to the food chain have been slightly less direct.

Matt, the mountain man, taught me backpacking, cooking over a fire at ten-thousand feet, and fly-fishing. In one corner of my kitchen leans the small fishing rod with which I lured many a mountain trout out of the cold stream and into a nice warm frying pan. We had many happy wilderness adventures together. One not-so-happy one was when I left our cooking gear out in the rainy darkness and Matt tripped on it on the way back to our tent, falling on the tent and snapping the poles. Propping up a crumpled tent in the teeming rain in the middle of the night, though, wasn't what ended our relationship.

Dexter, the Cockney Englishman, belonged to the Hash House Harriers. Their slogan: "A drinking club with a running problem." It's an international running club that focuses as much on food and drink, mainly the latter, as any athletic endeavors. Dexter, a round-faced pixie kind of guy, bustled about my kitchen, preparing savory meat pies and cockles and mussels, which he downed with great tankards of ale. "You need music in this kitchen," Dexter's cockney tones rang out.

So, he went shopping, returning with speakers and wires that crawled around in my attic and hooked the kitchen up to my living room stereo. Dexter is off and running somewhere with the Hash House Harriers, but the music in my kitchen croons on.

Some of my beaux left cookbooks and recipes behind. Edwin the English professor presented me with a beautiful fifteenth-century "cookry boke." One of my favorite recipes I make at least once each year:

Garbage
Take fayre garbagys of chykonys, as the hed, the fete, the lyuereys, an the gysowrys; washe hem clene, an caste hem in a fayre potte, an casste ther-to freysshe brothe of Beef or ellys of moton, an let it boyle; an a-lye it syth brede, an ley on Pepir an Safroun, Maces, Clowys, an a lytil verious an salt, an serue forth in the maner as a Sewe.

Not only am I indebted to various former lovers for many of the accoutrements of my kitchen, but to one I owe the fact that I own the kitchen and my house as well. Larry the lawyer handled my real estate trade, enabling me to move into my current home.

While I was writing this, my real honey-bunny ("Don't call me your honey-bunny in print," he said testily) served me a delicious crab and salmon salad on a bed of arugula and curly lettuce accompanied by a dish of toast points and *chèvre* along with a goblet of vintage Calistoga. He's still in my kitchen, and that's the best addition of all.

Women in Morocco

Up Against the Wall
But Laughing together

The smells of spices, hot coals, and sizzling food tantalized my nostrils. As I walked around the Jemaa el-Fnaa, the enormous plaza in Marrakech, a woman in black slipped in beside me. Surrounding us were jugglers, fortunetellers, acrobats, child boxers, snake charmers, and transvestites. All this receded as the woman in black stared deeply into my eyes. I said something to her in French, but she answered in a mixture of French, Arabic, and English. Totally covered from head to foot, only her penetrating eyes and etched cheekbones were visible. She stood so close to me that I could feel her breath and smell the scents she wore on her body. She might have been, probably was, both thief and prostitute. Yet, somehow I liked her and trusted her immediately. We both made some joking references to ourselves as women in a male-centered world. "Women are zero in Morocco," she hissed, forming a zero with her thumb and first finger for emphasis.

"I heard the king is making good reforms," I said.

"The king doesn't know what is really going on here. His people keep the truth from him. It is really terrible here for women. My husband was a kif addict, beat me, and knocked my teeth out." She opened her mouth and snapped her false teeth. "I get arrested for trying to sell things in the plaza. Now I'm pregnant. In addition to everything else, my ex-husband was a bisexual and HIV positive. I live in the medina. My son is in Italy."

"Why don't you get out of here?" I asked.

"I have no visa, no money. I'm not allowed to speak to tourists or sell anything without a license. I could never get one." Her bloodshot eyes teared up. She slipped an obviously fake silver bracelet onto my wrist. A hustle, no doubt, but a worthy one. I slid three-hundred dirham, about thirty dollars, into her hand. She was doing what she could to survive. On the edge of the crowd, a police car appeared. When I turned back to her, she had evaporated into the dusk of the teeming plaza.

One of the main reasons I travel is to attempt to understand people, who they really are, how their lives move along. This was certainly true for me in regard to Morocco. I had long been intrigued by this mainly Muslim, North African country's complexity and mysteries.

There were so many stories, so many views. At the center of the puzzle for me were, of course, Moroccan women. Somehow, I feel that by exploring women's lives in other cultures, I'll come to understand our conundrums here in the United States. In the last fifty years, so much has changed, but so much hasn't. I wondered how women managed today in a Muslim culture that had one foot in Europe and reached out eagerly to American tourism and business.

Statements I'd heard or read sang in my head:

"Wear loose long dresses that cover your arms. You'll feel more comfortable," advised a friend who had been to Morocco.

"Morocco has its dark side. You go to a beach and there are only male children. I picture all the girls sulking at home, covered with scarves and long robes," warned another.

"The King has many wives—no one knows how many—as he's a virile man" was a refrain I was to hear echoed, perhaps with some slight envy, by both American and Moroccan men.

"Moroccan men can legally have four wives. They can divorce by simply throwing the woman out and filing for divorce," I read.

"Ah, but now the law has changed: The woman must agree to be divorced. She can refuse," corrected an educated Moroccan woman I met in Rabat.

"As a woman, Morocco is the most exciting place to be right now. We are changing everything. We don't care about the laws. We are dragging the men along with us," proclaimed a French expatriate woman physician who practiced medicine in Marrakech and was married to a Moroccan man.

A feminist perspective always informs my writing, travel, and studies, and so it did in Morocco. However, I must admit that my interest in this country was not just scholarly inquisitiveness. I enjoy a good couscous, and I had a longing to ride a camel into the sunset on the Dunes of Merzouga. Most of my life and in many parts of the world, including the Middle East, I've been a solo traveler. I enjoy having no barriers, no buffers between me and the culture in which I'm immersing myself. However, although I'd been eyeing Morocco as a travel destination for a number of years, I had been warned that it was not advisable to travel there alone. Several friends reiterated, "It's easier to travel in Morocco with someone, preferably a male companion. It's not that it's dangerous. You'll just be hassled less. Because of the culture, it will be easier to concentrate on what interests you with a man along." The unfairness of this annoyed me. Then, into my life entered a male photographer who seemed like he might be the perfect choice. He said, "Yes, let's go to Morocco." Maybe the years were mellowing me. I decided to visit Maroc *en couple*.

We flew from San Francisco to Paris, changing planes there for Casablanca. Even on the plane, the mixture of modern and traditional influences all over Morocco was apparent. Some Arabic-speaking women wore Western dress, including one in jeans. In contrast, upon boarding our flight, we came across a veiled woman in a white headscarf and black djellaba with a henna-patterned forehead and chin. She led a small boy by the hand who wore black-and-white-checkered pants and a starched white shirt. He stepped carefully in his shiny, brand-new wingtip shoes. My companion had never seen a veiled woman close up before and found it very strange. He winked at the boy who tried to wink back but could only manage a double-eyed version. We all laughed, including the woman, behind her veils, although she modestly averted her eyes.

Once on the ground in Morocco, speaking no Arabic, I found my French useful in communicating with our driver and hotel personnel. Moustapha, our driver and guide throughout the trip, met us as planned at the airport. A colleague had recommended him, and he made our visit superb and became a good friend as well. My companion was content to leave arrangements up to me. We both found the irony amusing, and it lessened my impatience with the need for a male escort. Occasionally, when I was being ignored, I would ask my friend to intervene. For example, in our car on one particularly hot day, I asked our driver, "Please, would you turn on the air conditioning?" He mumbled something about the cost. I poked my male companion for support.

"Moustapha, that seems like a good idea to me," he agreed. Immediately, dials were turned and cool air began to flow.

Once in Morocco, our first stop was the Imperial City of Rabat. After our long flight, we were enjoying the luxury of a five-star hotel, but I worried we were missing the real Morocco. At breakfast, sitting at the next table was an elegant Moroccan woman in her fifties, wearing the traditional headscarf but exhibiting one exceptional variation: Instead of the usual solid-color black or purple djellaba, hers called to mind the flamboyant colors of Yves St. Laurent. Around us swirled piped-in New Age music. Not all of Morocco is donkeys and ancient kasbahs.

I had been reading and asking about women's and girls' lives, their access to jobs and education, how much free choice they had about marriage. The facts kept contradicting themselves. My reading told me that out in the villages and countryside, illiteracy among girls and women is common. Only about one-third of elementary schoolchildren are girls. My sources noted that in high school and university, the percentages are even lower. However, as we walked around in the cities, through the park in Rabat and in other cities along our route, female students were an obvious presence. It was examination time for university students, who gathered outside to study. In fact, there seemed to be more female than male students propped up all around with their books and notes.

In Rabat, at a pottery factory, several young Berber women beckoned me over to them. We exchanged a few pleasantries. They giggled and hugged me. They told me, "We're from the Atlas. It's much better for us here than back home where the women do all the work and the men just hang around and smoke kif [hashish] all day. We want husbands our own age who don't smoke kif. For women, life is easier here than in the mountains." However, at our next stop, Fez, our guide told me: "Up in the Atlas Mountains, Berber women have more freedom."

In Fez, when we met our local guide, Absallam, I mentioned that I wanted to get to know a young family and visit a hammam. He arranged for me to meet a young couple who lived on the outskirts of town. Khalid and Karima were twenty-five and twenty-one, married since she was fourteen. On the ground floor of a primitive stone building, their apartment consisted of three tiled rooms: a small living room, a dark kitchen separated by a hanging bead curtain, and one other room. Khalid worked on the street selling shoes. They had three children: six, five, and two years of age. Khalid told me, "Our friends and us, we are always happy, joking. We love each other, we don't expect much from life. If we have enough food, a place to live, our family and friends, we feel lucky." His wife, Karima, smiled but didn't speak much French. So I conversed mainly with him and his sister-in-law, Leila, who was waiting to accompany me to the women's hammam.

The ritual of the hammam is central to Moroccan life because often there are no bathing facilities at home. But as I entered the dank, hot, and humid tiled bathing place with Leila, watching her greet all her friends, I quickly realized it was more than a place to bathe. Like our health clubs, it is a social center for both women and men. Children sat quietly while their mothers scrubbed them down. "Here, wear my slippers. Watch your step; the floors are slippery." Leila and I undressed, and she paid someone a few dirham to watch our belongings. Leila is a beautiful young woman with glossy black hair. In contrast to the other women, who were either naked or wearing simple cotton underwear, her gorgeous body was adorned by a pair of stylish black lace panties. My own practical travel underwear was humdrum in comparison, and my body definitely carried a few more years of wear. She led me to the third of three progressively hotter chambers; then she carefully laid a rubber mat on the floor for me to sit on while she filled five or six old black rubber buckets for us with both hot and cold water from spigots at the end of the tiled room. She showed me how to use the special soap made from a local mineral and another slippery substance with which to rinse our hair. We scrubbed each other's backs with a kind of loofah sponge, apparently offending an older woman who picked up a few coins from people for the same service. She had identified me as a potential client.

I asked Leila if she was in school. "Yes, I was in school, studying *informatique*, computer studies. But my father lost his job, so I've had to leave school."

"Do you want to marry?"

"My boyfriend died in an accident fourteen months ago. So, if I meet someone one day. Meanwhile, I live with my family." Walking down the lanes, teeming with people, back to her family's house, I was aware of how industrious and orderly this society appeared to be. Everyone has their role, their work, and practices appropriate behavior and manners.

Back in the apartment, Karima prepared the henna solution while we all sipped mint tea. She applied the design to the backs of my hands with a hypodermic syringe, minus the needle. The henna is black when applied, making me look like a carefully decorated cake. After crafting the design onto my skin, she sealed it with sugar water. "Wash it off in about one hour with soap and water." Later, when I did so, a lovely burnt-sienna design was left on my skin. It wore off after about five days. I learned that henna is about the only type of primping allowed for Moroccan women; no other makeup is permitted.

Leaving Fez and just before our final stop, Casablanca, we explored the famous red-walled market town of Taroudant, framed by the High Atlas peaks, sometimes called "Little Marrakech" with its souks and ancient mystique. On our first day there, I asked our guide about the best way to meet some local women. "You should visit the wall," he said. "When the women of the town are finished working at dusk, they gather at the wall." In the late afternoon, we walked down the road that circled the town. The men were sitting on benches and small walls near the street. Sullen and silent, they stared straight ahead without any apparent communication among themselves or others passing by.

However, far behind them, back up against the high twelfth-century wall, the color of melting mocha chocolate, seventy-five to one-hundred women were sitting. Gradually, I wandered closer to them. Instead of the tense silence that hung over the men's area, I heard giggles and chatter. I had been afraid to offend them by looking directly in their faces but, when I ventured a glance, they waved at me, grinned, and beckoned me over. I was greeted by lots of female camaraderie accented with flashes of gold teeth. A jolly, robust woman, who apparently enjoyed her own cooking, spoke with me in French. "Yes, I'm married," she responded as we talked. "But my husband works in France and only visits me one week each year." She gave a jovial slap to her thigh and translated her words into Arabic for her friends. Peals of women's laughter rang back and forth along the ancient wall. Apparently, the key to a happy life was a husband who lived somewhere else!

For the traditional perspective, throughout the trip, our driver Moustapha, a Moroccan Zorba, had a running joke with my companion. It started when he asked the driver if he stayed at the same hotels we did. His reply was, "No, I stay at six-star hotels." With a wink, he joked about having a woman in every town in addition to his four wives, the legally allowed maximum. The truth would be revealed on the final evening of our visit.

In Casablanca, our final stop, we met a French woman doctor from Paris who was married to a Moroccan. "Next time you are in Casa, you must come to my house. I will have friends over. You will see. Moroccan women are making enormous strides. Laws don't matter that much. Women work now, earn their own money, do what they want. The change in divorce laws is a big help. A man now needs a wife's permission to divorce her. Formerly, he could just throw her out. The men are left way behind, their heads reeling. Women are dragging them along into the changes. It's exciting to live in Morocco now to see these fast changes."

In contrast, the tired travel agent who had arranged our schedule, a woman in her forties, looked like she was about to collapse from exhaustion when she met us at our hotel for final payment. "I worked from 7:30 this morning. It's now 8:30 at night. I have an hour's commute by bus to get home. Life has not been easy. My mother died when I was two. My father didn't want me to have an education. I don't want to be married. Married women are not happy. I live alone. It's hard but better than marriage."

On our last night in Casablanca, Moustapha invited us to dinner at his home. His wife and grown daughter were there along with a young grandson. Moustapha was enjoying playing host and patriarch of a large well-furnished house. But there was some tension or sheepishness on his part, and I was curious about it. This was different from his demeanor on the road. His wife spoke only Arabic and his daughter some French, but little English. After dinner, we settled onto the large couches that encircled the room. Moustapha spoke to me confidentially: "I'll tell you something in English. I bought a big house so that I could have a second wife downstairs. But my daughter moved in with her family, and they stay and stay."

His daughter sneered and interrupted: "Second wife! Are you saying that again? It's just male egoism. Four wives! Men still like to dream about the way they want it to be." Moustapha looked like he wished we were still out on the road, not in his living room where the truth was perhaps being revealed in contrast to his ongoing joke with my companion throughout the trip about having four wives as well as a woman in every town at his "six-star" hotels.

I flip back through the pages of my notebooks. Images crowd my mind: One will, I hope, stay with me forever. We were driving at dusk on the road from the Roman town of Volubilis to Fez. We passed soft tan- and pink-quilted fields with strata of gray and rose clouds above. Bedouin tents were nested throughout the newly harvested fields. Silhouetted against the horizon was a tall female figure. With arms outstretched, she whirled and swayed, dancing to music from within herself or from the earth around her. As we sped on down the road, I realized she was a Bedouin woman celebrating some joy out there by herself.

    The scrawl of Arabic script on another page conjures up an afternoon when we were wandering in the souk in Marrakech. A man walked along with us, engaging us in conversation. He offered my companion one-hundred-and-fifty camels for me. I told him that I was insulted. I was worth more. In any case, I insisted, we wanted the offer in writing. He upped it to two-hundred, wrote it in my notebook, and shook my colleague's hand. I was pretty sure they were kidding, but for some time afterward, we still wondered if we'd see a moving van full of camels pull up to my house in San Francisco.

PART V
Many Ways to Be at Home

In the quest for the "best of all possible worlds" . . . .
I know also, said Candide,
that we must cultivate our garden.

—Candide, Voltaire

In Colette's Boudoir

At Home in a French Château

One of my husbands used to suggest to me, "When you're about fifty you ought to write a sort of handbook to teach women how to live in peace with the man they love, a code for life as a couple." Perhaps I am writing it now.

—Colette, *Break of Day*

Early one July, I was driving along the rolling country roads of the Varetz region of France on my way back to Paris after visiting friends in the Dordogne. Someone mentioned to me that I'd be passing near Castel Novel, the thirteenth-century castle where French writer Sidonie-Gabrielle Colette, known simply as Colette, had lived with her second husband, the Baron Henri de Jouvenel des Ursins. When I heard that the chateau was now a hotel, I thought I'd try to stay overnight there. Just east of Périgueux, I turned off the main highway.

Colette's passions for love and sensual pleasures as well as for her career as a writer have long made her one of my favorite writers—and role models. She is among the most renowned and honored French writers of the twentieth century. The first female member of the prestigious Académie Goncourt and a holder of the Grand Cross of the Legion of Honor, she was the first woman in French history to receive a state funeral. She published more than seventy-three books; the best known are *The Vagabond* and *Gigi*. Perhaps better than anyone, Colette's writing helps us to decipher the temptation and intoxication of love.

Castel Novel was the fourth of Colette's homes I visited over the years, including her birthplace in the small village of Saint-Sauveur-en-Puisaye in Burgundy, where the excellent *Musée Colette* opened a few years ago. In Paris, I stood outside her apartment at the Palais Royale, and I wandered through her home and gardens in the hills above St. Tropez. A small sign announced the entrance to the château, and I turned my rented Citroën into the long tree-lined driveway. Perfectly manicured gardens on all sides, edged by vineyards and backed by ancient forests, boasted every color of the rainbow. An aquamarine swimming pool glittered in the Limousin sun. Just ahead, like something out of King Arthur and Guinevere's lives, rose the crenelated towers and steep walls of a medieval fortified castle. The castle and its current owners, the Parveaux family, welcomed me hospitably. As I was checking in, I asked owner and director Monsieur Albert Parveaux, "Is it possible to stay in Colette's room? She is one of my favorite writers."

"Well, you may look. It's our most expensive accommodation," he replied, sending me off with a youthful member of the staff and keys to several rooms. We visited two different rooms, both of which were nicely furnished, comfortable, quiet, and cool. Then the young man offered to show me the tower. "It's called the honeymoon suite." The French term *lune de miel*–literally "moon of honey," like so much that is French, always makes me think of something to eat. My guide added, "This is the oldest part of the castle; it dates from the thirteenth century."

We wound up the spiral stone stairs into the castle keep, now an elegantly decorated bedroom suite. A four-poster bed with gossamer draperies was the centerpiece; high above me arched a turreted roof, and through the windows, I caught a breathtaking look at a three-hundred-and-sixty-degree view of the lush Limousin countryside. My guide mentioned that the rough-hewn stone walls thrust downward into the very rock foundations under the château where Roman coins have been found. I was tempted to select this elegant chamber as my boudoir, but not yet.

"At least I'd like to have a look at Colette's apartment," I said.

On the opposite side of the castle, we entered through a pale-blue door into a combination sitting room, raised bedroom, and separate bath, all done in blue-and-white wallpaper. On the walls, old photos of Colette's angular face with her penetrating dark eyes peered at me, surrounded by photos of her mother Sido and Colette's many feline friends. A round table stood in front of the small fireplace. I wondered if Colette sat exactly there writing. I pictured myself doing the same, as well as enjoying my croissants and coffee there in the morning. Up half a dozen steps was a huge bathroom with a one-hundred-and-eighty-degree view from its expanse of windows. I imagined sitting in a hot bath in the large claw-foot tub and surveying the countryside. Returning to the salon, my guide swept back the lace curtains and pointed my way out to the balcony. I sighed contentedly as I thought of Colette sitting upon it, dreaming and writing while, like me, musing over these same fields and hills.

Returning to the front desk, I told M. Parveaux I would take one of the less expensive rooms next door to Colette's suite. With the smallest of bows, a nod of his perfectly coiffed head, and a well-tailored tweed stretch up the mahogany rack, he presented me with a key. Along with it, he produced a seemingly out-of-character wink. Carrying my luggage upstairs, the young porter placed my key in the lock of Colette's suite. I said, "No, no, I'm taking the room next door," certain that he had misunderstood my French.

"No mistake." He grinned. "Monsieur Parveaux is offering you this suite as a special surprise." The gesture pleased me, especially because, traveling alone as a single woman, I am careful not to allow myself to be treated unfairly. I had half-suspected that the director felt I wasn't important enough to be permitted to use her suite. Colette would have enjoyed this satisfying outcome.

After a relaxing swim in the Olympic-size pool at the foot of the opulent gardens, I went up to change for dinner. But first I sat on the third-floor terrace of

Colette's boudoir, collecting my thoughts and enjoying an aperitif, the cooing of the doves, and the blue-gray of dusk falling over the Limousin mountains.

It was a mild summer evening, and dinner was served at a beautifully appointed table on the terrace just in front of the château overlooking the gardens. A sophisticated Parisian journalist, ponytailed and bespectacled, sat at a table on one side of me. Eavesdropping as I always do when alone at meals, I heard him in an intricate discussion with Director Parveaux about an upcoming article concerning Henri de Jouvenel, Colette's second husband and the former owner of this château. At a table on my opposite side sat an American couple in their sixties from Long Island. They told me they were touring several châteaux for their honeymoon.

My meal began with a lobster mousse followed by a mixture of wild mushrooms, then roasted breast of duck, which was accompanied by what the menu described as a *filet de navets et ragoût de chou rouge* (turnip fillet and red cabbage). Finally, I relished a steamy orange-flavored soufflé. The sommelier recommended a delicious local Bergerac wine, Château la Jaubertie, Reserve Mirabelle 1996. When I'd skimmed the *Guide Michelin* earlier, it promised that Castel Novel's kitchen offered "traditional cuisine prepared with fresh ingredients from the Limousin countryside, complemented by Cahors, Bergerac, and vintage Bordeaux." They delivered and more.

Back up in my suite, I fussed, twisted, and ruminated, unable to sleep for more than a few hours. Even though I had visited several of Colette's homes, this was the first time I'd slept in her bedroom. In this château, she and her husband entertained family as well as literary and political friends. Henri composed his editorials for the celebrated Parisian newspaper *Le Matin*. She wrote several of her novels here and then interrupted her writing at age forty to give birth to little Colette. Henri and Colette's relationship was passionate and often tumultuous, especially due to his infidelities and Colette's seduction of her sixteen-year-old stepson, Bertrand de Jouvenel, whom she said she "taught to be a man." Ghosts of passion floated around me.

I went in and out of dreams about her life. Lines from her writing ran through my brain. In a letter, she described her blossoming love for Jouvenel: "I love this man, he's affectionate, jealous, unsociable, and incurably honest." In *Break of Day*, an autobiographical novel written some years later, she wrote: "Many stretches of the road have been completed and left behind. A castle inhabited for a moment has melted into the distance." The pure passion—lust, love, or a mixture—for a new lover is one of life's purest joys and not to be avoided, even if later, like the drop of an enormous ocean wave, the aftermath knocks the breath out of you. Like Colette, I appreciate the wonderful love and adventures I enjoy as I travel through my life. They are to be relished in the moment or longer and treasured as memories.

In the morning, I ate my breakfast from a silver tray: flaky croissants, *pain au chocolat*, toasted baguette, homemade jam and applesauce, freshly squeezed orange juice, and robust coffee. From the balcony, the surrounding countryside was peacefully hazy with soft mists. It was apparent that a sunny Limousin day would soon follow. Yes, castles, like love, inhabited even for a while along our stretches of road, are always to be treasured and savored.

Cuba

MACHISMO AND FEMINISM TOGETHER AT LAST?

"*Manuel, you did not take out the garbage. You are under arrest!*"

Ever since I heard about the "Family Law," I wanted to visit Cuba. I was curious to see firsthand a society developed by a macho-looking, bearded Latino who called himself a feminist and pushed such a law through early in the Revolution. Cuba's "Family Law" makes it illegal for a husband whose wife works outside the home not to participate in an equal share of the housework. In fact, a wife can perform a citizen's arrest on such a loafer.

In 1998, when the United States restricted visits to Cuba by U.S. citizens, one legal way to travel there was as part of a humanitarian group delivering educational or medical materials. You could fly in from Cancun, Mexico, or a Canadian airport. I joined Global Exchange, a San Francisco humanitarian 501(c)(3) nonprofit organization. As a women's rights advocate, I was especially interested in learning about the lives of Cuban women directly from the source. As a college professor, I entered the country bearing used laptops and other teaching materials. We flew in from Cancun. Our plane departed twenty hours later than scheduled. Rooms were scarce in Cancun, so a dozen of us ended up sharing one room just to have a place to relax.

Finally, we arrived. Approaching immigration control, I felt nervous. I thought about the warnings American friends had given me about the trouble I'd be in if I let Cuban authorities stamp my passport. I'd heard stories about needing to slip dollars into your passport as a bribe, about being taken into small rooms and interrogated, about communist rigidity and dangers. I took a deep breath and handed over my passport. The agent grinned at me and delivered an accented, "Welcome to Cooba," and before I could sputter, "No stamp, please," he imprinted only the loose slip of paper that was the visa form I'd received on the short flight over from Cancun.

On the twenty-minute taxi ride into central Havana, I saw American cars from the Fifties chugging along the road: canary-yellow Chevys, cherry-red Fords, lavender Plymouths—cars in bright shades U.S. car manufacturers never dreamed of. Dotting the highway were billboards: "Support the Revolution." "Believe in Fidel." "The People Will Triumph." "Think Soberly and Deeply."

Large numbers of women and girls stood on every corner. "Why are all those women hitchhiking?" I asked my cab driver.

"It's the law," he replied. "Everyone must pick up passengers. Gas is scarce, and we help each other out." I saw young schoolgirls hitchhiking by themselves. "Of course it's safe," he added, in answer to my unspoken question.

Spandex and miniskirts were everywhere, and I felt especially frumpy with my money-belt bulge under my shirt. Because U.S. banks don't trade with Cuba, my credit cards and American checkbook were worthless. So, the Yankee dollar was the currency of choice.

During one month in Cuba, I traveled by bus over much of the central and western part of the country, visiting schools and clinics, farms and villages and work projects. I talked with diverse people, trying to get a more balanced picture of a small country that continues to function despite the billions the United States government spends every year to annihilate its government and social system. I wanted to see especially how women were living and working in this unique society. Was it as terrible or as ideal as I'd heard?

My first morning in Havana I visited, on a bus with others, a community on the outskirts of the city, La Güinera, which some years before had been one of the worst slums in the country, festering with drugs, prostitution, hunger, and crime. Leaving the center of Havana behind, we passed through narrow streets where tiny houses and shacks leaned upon one another. A member of the Women's Federation, who accompanied us, said that about twenty-four-thousand people, six-thousand of them children, lived in the eight square-kilometer area we were about to visit. We climbed off the bus and entered the daycare center where four women in their twenties and thirties greeted us.

201

"This is a women-run project," Fifi, the director, said. "It all started with a communally-run daycare center so that women could hold jobs. Their idea grew, and soon an experimental project developed, supported by the government. Materials and training are supplied to people, teaching them to rebuild their houses, schools, stores, and clinics. In turn, they teach and help others to do the same. The crime rate has been cut to a negligible level. Former convicts lead productive lives. We all help each other out." I learned that professionals receive leaves from their regular jobs to add their skills to projects, like La Güinera, that exist all around the country.

Later, I wandered around on the streets. Two rough-looking guys I would normally cross the street to avoid were helping some children paint a fence. On another corner, we passed a makeshift meat stand. Several young black men waved at me from behind the counter. One of the women told me, "They're very active in this community. They used to be in prison. They were tough guys we call *guapos*. Now they are rehabilitated, and they work along with children, women, and the elderly, painting, building things, and supervising open markets."

As we walked up and down the streets, I noticed a particular kind of two-story building that appeared every ten blocks or so. "That's the community doctor's house. Each section of the community has its own doctor." I mentioned how clean the streets seemed. "We have a 'garbage patrol' organized through the environmental program in the schools. If children see anyone littering or throwing garbage on the street, they take it to that person's front door and hand it to them."

Back at the community center, one of Fifi's colleagues explained that this project had many levels: "For example, in the workers' dining room, we have a 'school table' where we teach people table manners and conversational skills. Just changing the environment, the buildings, does nothing. You have to change people's behavior, attitude, and manners. Everyone is encouraged to get as much education as possible. Children are urged to stay in school. There are special schools for hearing problems or behavior problems, for example. Adults go to evening school. Our community has its *Declaration del Arbol*, which means a community is like a tree with many limbs." She added, "Because the leaders are women, men don't feel so threatened."

As we said our goodbyes, Fifi added with a smile: "You know, *guapo* means bully and tough guy, but it also can mean beautiful and handsome. Here in Cuba, some men are *guapo*s, but women can be *guapas*. And in our community, our *guapos* become beautiful!" On my way out, I saw a notice on the wall that La Güinera had won an award from the United Nations in the category of a community project that especially helps women and children.

One day on the way to Trinidad in south-central Cuba, about five hours from Havana, I visited an organic farm. The director, Alice, an agronomist and trade union leader in her thirties, greeted us. "This project is called *las Marianas* after Castro's women's brigade. It is organized through the Federation of Women and run by an all-female staff. The goal is to train women to move from low-level jobs like housecleaning to better jobs and improve their lives." She pushed back a strand of black hair, her pink-pearl nail polish and silver hoop earrings flashing in the sun.

"We use organic insecticides, like extract of tobacco. It takes time to dab this extract on the plants." Alice smiled as a loudspeaker played Cuban jazz across the fields. "We enjoy our work." She grabbed a handful of soil, which she caressed and sniffed. "It's compost made from leftovers of sugar mills." Her dark eyes flashed with enthusiasm as she looked out from under the brim of her straw hat. "We sell to the city market directly: eggplant, guavas, tomatoes, garlic. The women here are in their thirties, mostly married, average of three children. The women find this work more rewarding than cleaning houses because they see that people are waiting for the food they raise. We see the trucks go out full and come back empty. There is good childcare here. We work the land ten hours a day, seven days a week. Each woman has two days off. We must work that much because people eat every day. We have a beauty parlor here, too."

One evening in a small town about one hour from Havana, I attended a meeting of the Committee for a Democratic Revolution, the municipal level of the government. Here I met Maria, head of the local branch of the Women's Federation, which represents women's interests in the three-tiered governmental system: municipal, provincial, and national. Maria's well-coiffed blonde hair, trim black-and-white suit, gold earrings, and eye makeup contrasted with the pale-blue chipped paint of the Women's Federation meeting hall. "Yes, forty percent of elected officials are female, but men are still macho," she informed me." "I practice law. Now that I'm divorced, I'm free. Men still want women to serve them. They still want to be kings. They haven't changed very much. However, from the beginning, the Revolutionary Committee was concerned with the improvement of women's status in society."

A young black woman, around twenty years old, joined our conversation. A successful athlete, she was studying to be an engineer. "I also love to play classical piano," she said.

"What are your dreams?" I asked.

"To be the best I can: construction engineer, athletics, music. And to travel like you."

The enthusiasm for learning among young people and the self-confidence of the young women especially impressed me throughout my travels in Cuba. The government had even established an active education campaign to combat teen pregnancy and sexually transmitted diseases. One afternoon while visiting a homeopathic clinic, an eleven-year-old girl who was part of a health education class asked the two of us, "Do you know about safe sex? I know that I must be careful not to get pregnant until I am over twenty. My uterus won't be ready to have babies until then." Because we were well beyond any risk of pregnancy, we were a bit amused by her directness, but her sincerity was impressive and a tribute to the Cuban education program beginning in youth regarding health and reproduction.

One day, we visited a college preparatory high school out in the country. As we entered a lab, our host and guide greeted us. Her curly red hair and blue eyes matched her open manner and self-confidence. A seventeen-year-old premed student, she showed us around the lab, where she and a group of others were conducting research on homeopathic remedies for skin infections, hypertension, anemia, and diarrhea. These students would be pharmacists and doctors. Even though Cuba has only two percent of Latin America's population, it trains more than twelve percent of Latin American physicians.

Unlike what we in the U.S. might expect, I traveled freely on my own throughout Cuba. I found people open, even eager, to speak with me when they learned I was an American. Never once did I experience any hostility or apprehension. On the University of Havana campus, I got into a discussion with some students who were sitting out on the lawn. "Cubans are sophisticated enough to differentiate between the American people and their government," they said. "Americans think we are imprisoned, but we feel that Americans are imprisoned by their ignorance. We say that the U. S. has so much opportunity, but Americans don't have the tools to take advantage of it. Cubans have the tools but not the opportunities. Cuba is not one man. You know, if there were an election tomorrow, Fidel would win. But the U.S. government wouldn't believe the results anyway."

The students I met seemed better read and more

aware of world issues than most of my students back home at the college where I taught. Some women students I spoke with studied in the Center for Gender Studies and told me it was well supported and popular. We all exchanged email addresses so we could stay in touch.

Over coffee one afternoon, a Cuban-American recording studio owner said to me, "I've had many Cuban musical groups come to the U.S. Out of one hundred, maybe two people defected. But, you know," he added, "there's a certain greed in human beings. I don't think socialism can work alongside capitalism. People want what others have. Castro had a nice idea to create an egalitarian society where everyone has their needs met. I'm not sure he'll be able to carry it off. Probably he shouldn't have nationalized private individuals' property. He pissed too many people off. A socialist country has to be surrounded by other socialist countries. And they don't exist anymore. Maybe China, but that's a very different situation. Cuba is not really communist. Castro wasn't interested in Communism or the Soviets. He just wanted to make a social revolution work. The U.S. policy drove him toward the Soviets." He added, "Cuba is a great place to raise children. The people here have good ethics; they are never vulgar; they have real family values."

On another day as I was riding in a cab along the Malecón, Havana's broad oceanfront boulevard, huge waves crashed over the seawall. The driver dodged walls of water breaking across the road and maneuvered his 1957 orchid-colored Chevy around the seawater spouting from the manholes. Outside the high-rise tourist hotels, instead of armed guards, young girls in spandex and sequins stood waiting, I realized, not for a bus. With foreign tourism replacing sugar as the main crop, prostitution was returning after a forty-year hiatus. Tourist dollars pay for education, health care, sports, and social security. They also bring sex tourists whose dollars offer young girls a more glittery life—at least for one night—than this social experiment of a society provides them. *What is the solution?* I wondered as I recalled the words of my recent conversation with the Cuban-American recording studio owner: "People want what others have. A utopian social experiment can only work in isolation or supported by societies with similar values and economic systems."

A joke someone told me that illustrates the lopsided economics is about a Cuban doctor who wakes up in the middle of the night and tells his wife he had the most wonderful dream. "I dreamed that I was a doorman at the Hotel Nacional." One night's tips in such a luxury hotel that serves foreigners generally would exceed the average physician's monthly salary of $97.

On my last night in Havana, after a dinner alone in a *parador*, a restaurant in a private home, I was wandering around on dark back streets trying to find a taxi. Suddenly, a man ran up toward me from behind. I thought, *Oh, no, not again*—as I'd been mugged twice back in California—and pulled my purse close to my body. He chattered away in speedy Cuban Spanish. I said loudly, "*no*," having no idea what he was saying to me. He switched to English: "Eets alright," he insisted, smiling at me, "women are safe in Cooba!" Apparently, he was asking if I needed assistance.

On my last day, an American friend, a woman who has lived and worked in Havana as a freelance journalist for fifteen years, drove me to the airport. Halfway there, a siren and blinking lights startled us, and a uniformed policeman motioned us to the side of the road. Images of life imprisonment and torture flickered through my mind, which wasn't all that clear after the mojitos and salsa dancing of my last night in Old Havana. The cop walked up to the driver's side and tipped his cap. He spoke to my friend for a minute or so, then smiled at us and left. "What was that about?" I asked.

"He noticed my license plate is hanging loose, and he didn't want me to lose it. But mostly he wanted to wish us a Happy International Women's Day. All police officers are instructed to pass this greeting on to every woman they meet today. Some police state, eh?"

Flying through the clouds, back to the powerful neighbor to the north, I recalled an afternoon I'd spent in the small town of Remedios, one of Cuba's oldest, dating from 1514. Its labyrinthine streets were created to deter pirates' attacks. Trying to find my way back to the main plaza and my bus, I asked an elderly woman for directions. Ana, a widow, invited me into her home. Inside her cozy and spotless house, she served me a glass of ice water, the best refreshment she could provide. Because my Spanish is minuscule, we each sat in a rocking chair and rocked together for a while in silence. Finally, when it was time to leave, we hugged. "*Hermanas*. Sisters," she said. I repeated, "*Hermanas*."

During the flight home, I was reading Cristina Garcia's novel, *Dreaming in Cuban*, about three generations of Cuban women, a family divided geographically and politically by the Cuban revolution and the United States embargo. A Cuban-American who had been visiting his mother leaned over and said to me with tears in his eyes, "*Cuba, qué es linda, no?*"

I nodded. "Yes," I said, "Cuba is beautiful."

As the plane carried me home, I thought about the various experiments over the thousands of years of human existence to create and maintain an equitable and humane society. Along the way, human nature hasn't changed, and perhaps that is the key. Maybe it's human nature that is sluggish in evolving.

Mongolia: Amazons and Horses

WAY OUT IN OUTER MONGOLIA

"Best keep your shirt on. We milk everything here." My local Mongolian guide was only half joking of course. We both had a good laugh on this first day of my month-long visit to Mongolia, which is really Outer Mongolia, Inner Mongolia being part of China.

Through my childhood, the phrase "It's like going to Outer Mongolia" has intrigued me. Where was Outer Mongolia, I wondered, and what was it like? Later, when I learned that this is one of the world's most remote lands, populated by horse people, I started investigating how to arrange a visit. I've been a horsewoman all my life, starting with riding lessons at age seven, later working with top trainers and learning the rare nuances of training "park" and gaited horses, and finally, training a unique mare who won national championships two years in a row. Horses have always been a major part of my life and are in my deepest psyche.

In addition to Mongolia's remoteness, uniqueness, and horse culture, another special attraction was that July, the planned date for my adventure, coincided with the annual spectacular celebration of the "three manly sports": wrestling, horse racing, and archery during the Naadam Festival. Even better from my viewpoint was that women now participate in the latter two competitions.

But there was still another intriguing mystery that drew me to Mongolia. Since the time of Genghis Khan and earlier, these people have been the world's best horsemen—and women. Homer, as well as the fifth-century BCE Greek historian Herodotus, described fierce women warriors who were superb horsewomen and archers. They were said to have lopped off their right breasts to be able to better handle their bows. Sarcophagus carvings actually illustrate this odd practice. In ancient Greek, *amazoi* meant "without a breast."

I'd read of a remarkable archaeological dig that had unearthed an ancient burial site, dating from the sixth to fourth century BCE, that consisted only of women's remains along with weapons, jewels, a saddle, and other artifacts indicating that these women were warriors and of high status. Careful study of their leg bones, which were oddly curved, suggested that the women had spent much of their lives on horseback. Furthermore, their right arm and shoulder structure was more highly developed than the left, like that of an archer might be. In addition, DNA extracted from these bones has found matches in women living in isolated areas of Mongolia, especially in Uvs *aimag*, or province, the most remote and least visited in Mongolia, way up in the northwestern corner bordering Siberia. This was my ultimate destination. As a scholar of feminist history as well as a horsewoman, I was very excited about what I might find during the expedition—maybe even descendants of the mythical Amazon women, although I didn't expect to find any single-breasted women.

And now here I was in Ulaanbaatar, the capital of Mongolia, land of the horse people. Mongolia is a chunk of the earth sandwiched between Russia and China. It's twice the size of Texas with a population of fewer than three million. Mongolia has been inhabited for more than eight-hundred-fifty-thousand years. Genghis Khan ruled over the Mongol Empire, the largest contiguous land empire in history. Known as "Super Father," with more than sixteen-million descendents still today, he was the Mongol conqueror.

On the four-hour flight from Ulaanbaatar, our twin-engine plane had flown low enough so that we could see snowy mountains smoothed with age and weather. Also visible were shadings of blue and dark patches of green forest stands, their own secret small kingdoms remote from the outside world, along with lakes, herds of horses and sheep, and lonely *gers*, the Mongolian word for the Russian *yurt*, sitting alone like small molded cream-cheese structures and surrounded by hundreds of livestock—sheep, goats, yaks, and horses.

The people who would be our drivers and guides for the next several weeks greeted us at the small airport, and off we went on the first of many wild jeep rides in old Soviet jeeps. My driver had a Rolling Stones sticker on his back window with Mick Jagger's tongue hanging out. It suited his driving style. Suddenly, he would look up a hill, veer off the path, then climb the hill, wheels spinning, sand and dirt flying. We'd leap madly off the edge at the top of the hill and bounce our way back down to the path. This was his idea of a shortcut. After a several-hours-long, bouncy, breathtaking, and varied jeep ride (there are no roads in most of Mongolia, just animal trails and dry river beds) during which we sped past *ovoos*—shamanist sites of worship, typically with offerings of blue silk, money, food, and the ubiquitous vodka bottles—we arrived at our home for the night, *Üüreg Nuur* (lake).

With amazing speed, our hosts set up a dining tent and individual tents and prepared the meal. Just as we all were seated at the dinner table, the sky darkened, and the wind whistled and sent the sides of our dining tent pulsating. Sand filled the air and our mouths instead of food. "It's a sandstorm," I said to the others, thinking I was making a joke. But it was no joke. For the next several hours, the winds and sand pounded us. After staggering against the sand-whipped winds back to our shelters, we huddled in our small individual tents, the stakes firmly pounded into the ground by our careful guides. Occasionally, I'd risk the incoming swirl of sand to peek out at Üüreg Nuur, one of the world's largest lakes, now with huge waves like a wild sea, racing one after another to the lakeshore just below our camp. Finally, when the winds subsided, I ventured out of my tent and ran through the warm rain to the provision truck for a tepid OB beer, the local brew, curious to look around.

Almost simultaneously over the lake, two double rainbows appeared along with a full moon and a spectacular sunset. The crew dusted off the dining tent table, plates and food reappeared, and we all sat down to a meal made even more delicious by the wait. We'd been up since 4 a.m.

The local Mongolian outfit my small group traveled with kept us well cared for throughout the trip, which we experienced partly in old Soviet jeeps that broke down frequently and partly saddled up on horses that never broke down. The food, mainly rice and mutton, was plentiful and well prepared.

I had read about a Mongolian delicacy, marmots, which are roasted with hot stones in their bellies. I looked forward to sampling one, especially when I learned that the dirt mounds surrounding our camps were large marmot burrows. Sadly, on the second day of our trip, one guide warned us: "It's bubonic plague season. Don't eat any marmots, and don't go near dead animals." In one of the fairly grim tiny towns we visited, an old man sat next to me and chatted while I was resting on a wall. I thought he was hustling me. Later, a guide clarified, "He was giving you his special recipe for marmot, but wait until plague season is over."

The national dress for both men and women is the *deel*, which resembles a large overcoat, usually in shiny dark blue, rose, or green. Not only comfortable and warm, it is a sort of traveling toilet as the wearer needs only to bend down on one knee to enjoy some needed privacy. Definitely an animal-centered culture, the spacious land punctuated by steppes is also the home of large herds of horses, sheep, goats, camels, yaks, and cattle. The animals, even without the privacy of *deels*, enjoy a spacious bathroom. I learned to watch my step as "toilets" are everywhere. Migratory people, the Mongolians waste nothing, and animal dung is collected like firewood for heating and cooking. Outside each *ger* is a carefully stacked dung pile.

Living with their herds, Mongolians make dairy products which are a staple of their diet along with meat. As I stepped into my first *ger* as a welcome guest, carefully with my right foot first and moving counterclockwise as I'd been instructed, I sat on a cushion, and the family offered me my first *airag* or fermented mare's milk. This is a drink of choice, and I quickly developed a taste for it. Another staple is dried yogurt curd, mainly dipped in salt milk tea and gnawed on as a snack as well as offered as a gift to all visitors. I had come prepared with a supply of small gifts: postcards of San Francisco, pens, various pins, even energy bars as my other supply ran low. I gave away several T-shirts until I was getting close to finding it difficult to keep a shirt on. There were days when we fled on horse or jeep to escape locals running toward us bearing handfuls of yogurt curd offerings because our own reciprocal gift supply was fast disappearing.

Early in the trip, one *ger* we visited had a typical stove, many rugs and cushions, a gorgeous saddle with a red-velvet seat, silver embossed studs, and soft old well-oiled leather. A couple lived there with their four children (ages six months to eleven years) and sister-in-law. We all drank *airag* and got very jolly. We also played a game that involves changing positions to take another's place. I was not sure of the goal, but we all laughed a lot and had fun.

"We are happy to have you visit us because living in this remote area, we don't get to see strangers very often."

"Would you like to come to New York City or San Francisco?" I asked. I gave the mother a postcard of an aerial view of San Francisco.

"I may get somewhere else, but I'd never get to America," she said, apparently content with that.

I offered a few granola bars as a gift. "Is it for the night or the day?" the father asked, reminding me of how traditions are deeply entwined in this land, and even a small new object needed to find its correct place. I explained that it was a snack, probably for the middle of the day.

My years as a horsewoman were good preparation for this trip. At one point, the head horseman asked our translator to tell me that he admired my seat—and I knew he wasn't being rude.

Each day, we rode six to eight hours, alternating in a jeep when we wished. Because of my stiff hip, which I injured while training a young horse back in California, I requested a narrow horse and was offered a small chestnut mare. The Mongols love their horses but don't name them. Our Mongolian guide said, "We have too many—sometimes two hundred—to name."

Not much taller than ponies but surefooted with great endurance, Mongolian horses are never really trained in the sense that we in the West might expect. The morning ritual was that our horsemen mounted each one and galloped it around until he or she stopped bucking. Then they were handed over to each of us to mount.

"Tschou" is the word Mongolian horses most respond to. Sounding like a sneeze, it is their version of giddyup. I tried it, and it apparently made sense to my small but wiry chestnut Mongolian mare who eagerly forged ahead each time I half-sneezed at her.

As we rode along, the horseman riding nearest to me began singing what I recognized to be *khoomei*, the famous throat singing of this region. It's a technique that simultaneously creates high and low notes as though one person's throat has a harmonic chorus set up inside of it. I learned that Mongolian horsemen just naturally and un-self-consciously sing whenever the mood strikes them. The songs imitate the natural world in which they are so deeply intertwined: the sounds of water running in streams, the steady beat of horses' hoofs in dirt, or the sounds of winds coming over the steppes. Often, the songs are about horses and love. "My horse goes quickly as he knows I'm hurrying to my love" goes one popular song. At one point during the trip, I asked the men to teach me how to sing *khoomei*, but they refused. The traditional belief is that the vibrations can cause women to miscarry. I wanted to explain that this was not a concern of mine, but I dropped the subject. Later on, when I met with women from the Mongolian Women's

Federation, they said that women were now taking up the technique and forming their own female *khoomei* groups.

Every day, we witnessed life in the steppes as we rode past. A young shepherdess yelped and whistled as she guided her herd of about three-hundred sheep and goats. About fourteen years old, she was adept atop her well-kept bay horse on a red-felt saddle. The herding system seemed to involve the animals wandering up the hills and the young girl circling them on her horse and pushing them back down in an endless pattern.

What were women's options here, I wondered? While visiting one family, I was able to speak with the daughter, Nara, who was studying civil engineering in Irkutsk. Having received no sex education before she began to date, after two months she became pregnant. Her Mongolian boyfriend's mother was helping to raise the daughter. Her own father was a drunken soldier. "Women are more reliable. Men drink and don't give money for their children. It is easier for women to get jobs," she said. However, I learned that wages are very low. For example, a teacher earns the equivalent of $100 US/month and even a small apartment costs $200.

After about one week touring and visiting families and gorgeous steppes, at dinner, our group leader announced: "Tomorrow, the Naadam games begin!"

Early the next morning, way out on the steppes, we arrived at the Naadam Festival, where a Buddhist priest was leading the men in prayer. A group of women dressed in special purple and gold *deels* invited us into their large ceremonial *ger*. We joined them to form a circle of approximately thirty people. They served cookies, yogurt curd, candies, pickles, and tiny pieces of meat and asked us each to introduce ourselves, including our ages and number of children. Those with the most children got the most applause. Even though I had no offspring to report, saying that I was a teacher and writer gave me special status.

Offering our thanks and goodbyes, we left the tent to head over to the wrestling matches that were about to begin. I admired a woman's horse. Dressed in well-tailored jodhpurs and boots, she dismounted and offered me a ride on her horse over to the outdoor wrestling area where I reconnected with my group.

We were given the honored place in the shade. The haunting strains of classic Mongolian music settled the audience into a focused mood. We swayed to the ancient sounds of the horsehead fiddle (*morin khuur*), a dulcimer, zither, and *bishuur* (clarinet-like pipe). The thirty-eight wrestlers, we were told, begin with the Eagle Dance, modeling the free movements of regal birds. Wonderful to watch, the men were tall, muscular, lean, and wearing high black boots. My eyes were especially focused on their tiny red or blue shorts. The white embroidery along the edges accentuated their bronzed Herculean thighs. Contrasting with their shorts in blue or red, their off-the-shoulder long-sleeve shirts displayed their bare midriffs.

Unlike American wrestling, which is much more active, the men seemed to just lean on each other without much action as though they were in a trance or meditative state. Each match went on for about one hour with breaks provided by small children running out with wet cloths. "This wouldn't sell well in the U.S.," said one American in the audience. "They haven't done anything for forty-five minutes." I rooted for the one with the best, in my judgment, thighs and ass.

I snapped a photo of the winner drinking from the winner's goblet of *airag*, taking care to focus in on the milky dribble going down his chin. Back home, I submitted my photo to the "Got Milk" contest, but it was rejected on the grounds that the beverage was not cow's milk.

Later that day, we received some disturbing news. During the large national wrestling match in Ulaanbaatar, which was occurring simultaneously with the events we were attending, the challenger kicked the reigning champion in the balls, in a very unsportsmanlike way, and the match was held up while the poor guy was treated in a hospital. To everyone's delight, the champion returned and defeated his foe.

The famous horse races were the highlight for me. We drove over to the area where the race would begin. The jockeys were children, ages five to twelve, not surprising because children learn to ride almost before they can walk. Looking around, I saw no racetrack but learned that the race was cross-country. At a certain point, the cluster of perhaps fifty horses and children took off haphazardly and disappeared over the horizon. Covering about twenty miles in one-hundred-and-five-degree heat, most of them rode bareback, the young jockeys stuck to their mounts' backs like glue. We waited about two hours for the racers to return. The camaraderie was similar to tailgate parties as people visited with each other, shared food, and relaxed.

Finally, the first returning horse was spotted in the distance. It was organized chaos as each father caught the horse's bridle as his child crossed the finish line. Some horses returned riderless, so I imagined there was a system for parents to ride out and retrieve their kids. I marveled at the hardiness of these people, horses, and children. One father caught his daughter's bridle as her horse crossed the finish line first. The winner! The man, himself atop a prancing black stallion, was clearly a local hero, cheered on by the surrounding fans.

He was especially handsome: a classic Mongolian face with its high prominent cheekbones, chestnut skin with ruddy cheeks, straight flat nose, bright large dark eyes, handsome sculptured ears, straight proud posture, high forehead, and a direct gaze that focused on you for a long time. As people were milling about, we caught each other's glance. I asked to snap his photo with his winning child and horse. Then we stood smiling at each other. Outside of lingering glances, he and I had no common language. We exchanged names: "Ganhuig." "Diane." When I returned to my waiting jeep and driver, Ganhuig followed me. Oozing self-confidence, he climbed inside while his black stallion rubbed his head and neck on the outside of our jeep, much to the annoyance of my young driver. About fifteen of his male friends surrounded our jeep and laughed good-naturedly at Ganhuig's nerve, acknowledging his attraction for women as the local hero and Don Juan.

In other countries and earlier years, perhaps he and I would have had a tryst. But here on the steppes, I only could fantasize about leaping aboard his stallion and riding double, back to his *ger* somewhere in a fold of the surrounding grasslands. Erasing the likely realities of flocks of his children, his wife, and relatives from my fantasy, I thought about the complexities of removing all those layers of *deels* and other mysteries of Mongolian clothing. No zipless fuck, this, as I recalled Erica Jong's feminist classic, *Fear of Flying*, in which she described the sexual fantasy when "clothes vanish like gossamer." Buttons and zippers would open magically and layers of dusty *deels* would fly away. Because there would be no running water, I wondered if layers of sweat and dust would act as an aphrodisiac.

Instead, Ganhuig wrote his name and address in my notebook so I could send him photos, but of course, it was in Mongolian and Ganhuig bid me farewell.

A few days later, even though it was July, we awoke one morning to a world of heavily falling snow and freezing temperatures while at our highest camp at over seven-thousand feet. Our horses with their heavy coats pawed for grass beneath the snowy surfaces where they were tethered. Snow surrounded my small tent. All was white, cold, quiet. Just beyond, my gaze followed gray rocks as they climbed up a small rise, and just above them, silver, white, and black clouds crowned the horizon. A horse whinnied, breaking the silence. I slipped out of my warm

223

sleeping bag and stepped out into the frigid air of Uvs Province in northwestern Mongolia. Silhouetted against the white and gray, a prancing black stallion, neck arched, strained against the lead rope held by a young woman in red and green robes.

All during the day, like a mirage, this young woman, perhaps in her early twenties, drifted around the perimeter of our camp guiding a gorgeous jet-black stallion on a tether as he grazed, pranced, and cavorted. His long mane and tail flowed in the wind. At one point, she leapt on to his back and galloped in circles around our camp.

Our guides warned that perhaps she was looking to rob us, but somehow that didn't seem the case to me. Later in the day, I walked out and smiled at her. She returned the greeting. Tall with a proud strong posture and large intelligent eyes, she was tanned and rose-cheeked. Her face was stunningly beautiful. After some sign language, she gestured for me to follow her. I asked some of my fellow travelers to join us, but they were suspicious and declined. Leading her spirited mount, we descended the slope to her family's *ger*, set up beside a rushing mountain stream. In front, a baby, maybe a one-year-old, sat astride a small horse as though it was her rocking horse.

Her family invited me inside for the traditional salt milk tea, *airag*, and yogurt curd. It was very crowded, and the four or five men inside were clearly drunk. Vodka bottles were strewn all about the floor. It is said that the Soviets may have departed after their occupation, but they left the curse of vodka behind. The women stirred the salt milk tea, politely smiled at me, and nodded. We communicated with hand gestures. "Thank you." "Goodbye." After a time, I thanked my young friend and prepared to return to my camp. The girl threw her arms around me and held tight, her eyes filled with tears. Without words, I understood that she wanted to escape from this desolate existence.

Do myths have shelf lives? Do they wither as centuries go by, and cultures no longer accommodate what might have been? Like a Candide, in my ongoing search for the best of all possible worlds, had my dream of Amazon women fallen off its pedestal? Perhaps not, because I did meet an amazing young horsewoman out there on the steppes and we had somehow connected.

Even though I didn't bring my young friend home with me, my Mongolian memories traveled with me: a lone horseman at dusk hurriedly trotting off across the plains into the space of steppes that is Mongolia; an isolated *ger* surrounded by marmot dens with their scattered bones; the taste of *airag*, dried yogurt curd, salt milk tea, homemade vodka; the smells of wet sheep-wool felt, the smoke of burning dung, *ger* beetles, cool grass, dry rugs; and the sounds of *khoomei* singing accompanied by horsehead stringed instruments.

Above all, I think of the young horsewoman I met high in the mountains who seemed to me to be from another time. Perhaps the lost culture of the Amazon women still has descendants out here in the Altai Mountains of Mongolia.

Dinner in Dushanbe, Tajikistan

AFGHAN WOMEN'S RESILIENCE AND RESISTANCE

"Please speak out about these crimes. But tell not just about the suffering, but also about the successes, how we are resisting," said Halida, a math professor from Kabul who ran secret schools for girls inside Afghanistan throughout the repressive Taliban regime. Dressed in a gunmetal-gray long dress, her resolute features contrasted with her delicately embroidered white headscarf. She was one of several hundred Afghan women with whom I spent a week in Tajikistan, not far from the Afghan border. Getting to know them and hearing their stories taught me a lot about our shared humanity and the human ability not only to survive but to continue to savor life.

It was June 2000. The Taliban were still in power in Afghanistan. Their treatment of women seemed to me the ultimate in man's inhumanity to women—imprisoned in their houses, denied education or the ability to work, forced marriages, beaten and even stoned to death—and I wanted to do something to help.

While I was living and teaching college in France, I met a group of Afghan women who were political refugees. One of them said, "We're organizing a conference for Afghan women in Dushanbe, Tajikistan, on the Afghan border. Can you assist us?" Paris was in the full glorious bloom of early summer; all around me were color and flowers, women in their summer dresses, leisurely meals at sidewalk cafes. I'd be swapping this for a Soviet-style gray-cinderblock experience. Still, I agreed. None of us were quite sure what awaited us there.

Along with some French women, we worked out the complex details of visas and flight routes, which included stopping overnight in Moscow en route to Dushanbe. I was apprehensive about entering an area of the world that was very much a war zone, but my colleagues assured me that if things seemed to be going awry, we would leave quickly. Once there, we were to meet with more than three-hundred Afghan women who had escaped across the Afghan-Tajik border. Our goal was to help them write "A Declaration of the Essential Rights of Afghan Women," based on United Nations documents. We hoped that major elements of our work would eventually be incorporated into the soon-to-be-created Afghan Constitution and that our Declaration would be signed by world leaders, including then-U.N. Secretary-General Kofi Annan and then-U.S. President Bill Clinton.

Upon our arrival from Paris via Moscow, at the tiny Dushanbe airport, several hundred Afghan schoolchildren in red, gold, and purple traditional embroidered clothing, as well as women and men, greeted my friends and me with roses and floods of tears. One woman threw her arms around me. "We are so happy to see you. We thought no one knew this was happening, that no one cared about us."

For the next five days, we met in a large conference room jammed with hundreds of women and a sprinkling of men, in our simple cement-block hotel.

"Persecution of women is a method to install terrorism in order to paralyze society, to create a submissive society." Khalida Messaoudi, Deputy from the Algerian government, opened the conference with these words. A charismatic woman in her early forties, her slight build belied the power of her ongoing work for women's rights. Proceedings moved slowly as all speeches and statements had to be translated from Dari, the North Afghanistan language, to French and vice-versa. A tiny air-conditioning unit in one corner of the room made no impression on the hotter-than-one-hundred-degree humid air. I sat steaming in my dark yellow tunic top and long skirt. The Afghan women in patterned gray, black, and brown long dresses with contrasting red and gold headscarves didn't even seem to perspire. These women who were attending the conference had sufficient education and economic background to escape across the border. We learned later that hundreds of their less fortunate sisters inside Afghanistan had received word of our conference and met secretly to sign the petition, organize, and plan further rebellion. The burqa, the total body and head drape prescribed by the Taliban, makes an excellent covering for transporting secret messages within the women's community as well as food and ammunition to their men at the front.

After a short speech I gave as an American educator and writer concerned about the Afghan situation regarding women's rights, people lined up to speak with me. They expected that as one of the three Americans at the conference, I could work miracles. Their desperation made me wish that I could.

"Please help us. My family in Afghanistan is starving."

"My brother needs eye surgery. Can you help us get him to a hospital in France or the U.S.?"

"My sisters and mother have been taken prisoner by the Taliban. Please help me find them."

"Why can't America stop Pakistan from continuing to fund the Taliban?"

I met almost around the clock with women professors, doctors, engineers, and computer scientists. Their stories revealed to me what the civil society of Afghanistan has been and can be once again. Western news coverage of Afghanistan generally presents a picture of illiterate warlords and draped women, which makes it easy for us to dismiss their situation as hopeless. However, earlier, back to the sixties, Afghanistan was a progressive society. Women's equal rights were guaranteed by the Afghan constitution. In pre-Taliban Afghanistan, women, at least in the urban centers, were educated and active participants in the society. They comprised fifty percent of the civil administration, seventy percent of the teachers, forty percent of the physicians, and had fifteen-percent representation in the highest legislative body in Afghanistan—a larger number than in the United States.

One afternoon outside the meeting hall, the face of one woman especially intrigued me. As I looked at her on that sweltering day, Sophia, in a black dress and coat, formed a slight figure. Probably in her twenties, her gaunt face and dark hair peeked out from under her black-and-tan headscarf. Her large eyes had a tragic, almost hypnotic stare. I introduced myself in simple French and English. As we talked a bit, Sophia explained her situation: "My sister died three months ago. My husband is in southern Tajikistan, trying to find work. I am living with my brother-in-law and taking care of his three children." Before we parted, she invited me to dinner that evening at her family's home. Not thinking about possible risks, the opportunity to spend time with a family and get away from the hotel where we were staying appealed to me. I accepted.

About 8 p.m., her brother-in-law, Mohammed picked me up at my hotel. Dressed in tan slacks and a white shirt, he explained that his business, exporting flour and sugar, enabled him to support his family and to escape from Afghanistan over the border into Tajikistan. Making our way along the dimly lit, empty streets, as we neared each intersection, Mohammed flattened the gas pedal to the floor. We flew past the police, who were stationed on each of the four corners on every block.

"They are out each evening and stop anyone they

feel might give them a good bribe," he explained. A breakaway state from the former Soviet Union, Tajikistan's supposed democracy is at best corrupt and at worst very much a police state.

After about ten minutes, we parked beside a Soviet bloc-style cement apartment house. We walked up three flights of uneven and broken stairs in the pitch-black. Sophia, who met us out front, held fast to my hand and guided me up one step at a time. "No, there are no lights," they apologized. The sweat was running off me in the heat. It occurred to me that I hadn't told anyone from our group where I was going. We'd been warned not to wander around in the town at night. People were living under desperate conditions here. Was I about to be kidnapped? I thought about turning and running back down the stairs. But where would I go? I had no idea how to get back to the hotel.

Instead, the door opened to a brightly lit and spacious apartment, clean but sparsely furnished with overstuffed black-velvet chairs and a couch. A tiny elderly woman, hunched over with osteoporosis but still spry and cheerful, whom they introduced as *Apa* or Grandma, planted kisses on both of my cheeks. They all ushered me in, the children kissing and hugging me. We sat in the living room and talked. For a moment, now and then, a wave of intense grief would cover one face or another. Then that person would rejoin us in the moment, hospitable toward this new friend, eager to enjoy some momentary pleasure.

Apa brought out platters of her special chicken kebobs along with *qabili palau*, the ubiquitous and delicious Afghan rice dish, a mixture of raisins, lamb, nuts, and local spices, accompanied by fresh tomatoes, cucumbers, peaches, and watermelon. No one bothered about the flies crawling on the chicken nor the ants on the watermelon. These people have been through so much as refugees of war, bereft of a sister, a wife, and a mother, yet they relish moments of love and happiness, perhaps more than many of us remember to do.

After our meal, Apa settled onto the couch, and with strong arms and hands, pulled her twelve-year-old grandchild, Leda, into her lap. The grandmother wore a gauzy white head covering and was dressed in a neat black-and-white patterned dress. Her body was strong and wiry, her skin smooth, her eyes surrounded by dark circles. She seemed ancient, and I was surprised to learn that she was only seventy. For more than twenty years, she had lived under war: first Soviet attacks, then anarchy, now totalitarianism and exile.

The children were very bright, cheerful, and confident, and enjoyed showing off their English to me. They wore the typical jeans or pedal pushers and T-shirts like any child in the USA or Europe. Sophia's dark hair was pulled back in a bun, and she wore a simple black dress. Twelve-year-old Leda and I seemed to feel comfortable with each other, exchanging little winks and smiles. Conversation flowed easily. We talked about their current life and the lives they left behind as well as some of their pleasures like music and reading. They asked about my life and family. When they learned my family had been dead for some years, that I was single and had no children, their eyes misted over with sadness. "You must be lonely," they said.

After a few minutes, Leda took my hand. "Take me home with you. Please adopt me." I smiled, thinking she was teasing, but when I looked up at her family's faces, I could see that they all approved of the idea.

"Then you won't be alone," Sophia said. I told them I was very touched but didn't know if I could do this. As I was leaving, they pressed various gifts into my hands, including a beautiful woven blue-and-brown scarf. "To remember us."

"I'll send you gifts from the States," I promised.

"Sometimes packages get through," they said.

As I flew back to Paris and the following year returned to the United States, I continued to carry with me not only the scarf but a memory of how love and human fortitude prevail all over the globe in areas we barely know exist.

Postscript: I continue my work giving readings and photo screenings to raise money and awareness for the Afghan women, supporting Women for Women International, Afghan Women's Literacy projects, Afghan Education for a Better Tomorrow, and others. I have also stayed in touch with these dear friends. Leda is now married to an Afghan and living in England on a tenuous U.K. visa. The younger sister, Sweeta, is now a senior at the American University in Kabul and has kept in touch by email. I've been supporting her efforts to get a visa to move out and study abroad. She's very smart and hard-working, fluent in several languages, writes and publishes in English, and is a top student. Since the political and economic situation has severely worsened in Afghanistan, obtaining a visa is very difficult as tens of thousands of Afghans are hoping to do the same.

Hurrah! She recently wrote to say that she has successfully obtained a visa and scholarship to study for an M.A. in China and from there intends to apply for a U.K. visa.

At Home in Afghanistan

PEACE IS EVERYTHING

"Those are the Hindu Kush Mountains, the killer of Hindus," said the Afghan man seated beside me, pointing. We were on a flight from Dubai to Kabul and, through the window, I could see the flat desert of Iran and southern Afghanistan suddenly give way to barren blue-and-gray ridgebacks like the waves of a stormy sea. I wondered how stormy the political situation would be during my visit to this war-weary land. Twenty-four hours ago, as I prepared to leave for the San Francisco airport, a neighbor had called to say that another bomb had just exploded in Kabul. "Should you delay your departure?" she asked.

It was 2002, one year after the World Trade Center bombing and the subsequent fall of the Taliban. I was traveling to Afghanistan as part of a human rights delegation sponsored by the San Francisco-based organization Global Exchange. There were eleven of us, mainly young Afghan-Americans and me, a recently retired college professor. Our mission was to assess the state of Afghan culture and the arts and set up projects both immediate and long-term. Having worked for women's rights all my life, I planned to focus on that area.

I had never visited a war zone, however, and couldn't help feeling anxious. Small villages of stone and mud dwellings grew visible as we angled in toward Kabul Airport. Voices and nervous laughter grew louder as excitement mounted among the passengers. Many were Afghans returning home after absences of fifteen and even twenty years.

"I left when I was three," one man said, while another confided: "I'm afraid to get off. Everything will be so changed."

Our plane swept past bunkers and a graveyard of smashed planes and the cadavers of military aircraft. We were entering a land of lawlessness, anarchy, warlords, and twenty-three years of conflict—a part of the world where civil war and foreign invasions were more "normal" than peace.

We stepped off the plane into the "Country of Light," as Afghanistan has been called. A young Afghan-American traveling with us said: "I thought I wouldn't remember anything since I moved to the States when I was five, but now that I feel the air, I know I am home." Inside the terminal, young men in ragged brown garments who looked straight out of the Middle Ages pleaded to help me with my luggage to earn ten-thousand Afghanis, about twenty-five cents.

A van awaited us. "Don't worry that there are no seatbelts," said the driver. "I drive slowly." Then he floored it, racing up the wrong side of the divided street against the oncoming traffic. Indeed, there seemed to be no traffic rules or stoplights in Kabul. Traffic moved like spilled milk—anywhere space allowed.

Through the open window of our van, I bought the autumn 2002 *Survival Guide to Kabul* from a street child. "There's a lot to see, even if most of it is wrecked," it noted. On the way to our hotel, we passed bombed-out houses, stores, and even palaces. Near the center of the city, burned skeletons of buses were stacked on top of each other around the devastated former public transportation center. Women in blue burqas and street children begged at the windows of our van. Men with no legs, victims of mines, negotiated the streets on makeshift skateboards in the traffic, pleading for baksheesh, or money.

As we approached our hotel, I noticed the top floor had no roof, only jagged remnants left behind by a past shelling or bombing. Affecting nonchalance, I joked to the driver that I sure hoped our rooms would be on a lower floor.

Our guide suggested we visit Darul Aman Palace and the Kabul Museum first. We climbed into a minivan and bounced along through the dust on the remnants of a formerly paved street. From a distance, the palace looked appropriately majestic high upon a hill. Photos I had seen from the 1920s depicted an impressive three-story turreted edifice, but as we drew near, we realized that the palace walls were now pocked with cavernous holes. Security guards yawned as they waved us through the gate. At the front entrance, we came upon a young guard sleeping on the ground atop a red woven rug. A Kalashnikov lay beside him.

"Salaam," we said, hoping to sound friendly. Staring up at us, he rose slowly to his feet, rubbing his dark-brown eyes and running his fingers through his curly hair. In his late teens or early twenties, he would have been a heartthrob in any American high school. Our guide explained that we wished to visit the palace. The guard waved us in, and soon we were wandering through rooms that had once been grandiose but now lay in ruins. The large chunks of missing wall permitted panoramic views of the countryside: parched rolling hills backed by hazy blue mountains.

Curious about some fresh graffiti on one wall, I stopped and peered through a doorway. The smaller adjacent room was newly plastered and painted. Noticing my curiosity, the young guard motioned for me to follow him into the bathroom next door. It featured a sparkling new white porcelain bathtub. In hesitant English, he said: "A few weeks ago, bin Laden stayed here. They prepared these rooms for him." This couldn't be true—could it? Regardless, the notion that I might be staring at the world's number-one terrorist's recently used bathtub made my temples pound. I hoped that he wouldn't be bathing here today.

I was about to rejoin the others when the guard held out his Kalashnikov and pointed at the camera hanging around my neck. Curious to hold one of these infamous Russian weapons, I accepted his offer, cradling it carefully with my fingers far from the trigger. He snapped my photo with his weapon in my hands.

From there, we drove back down the hill to the equally battered Kabul Museum. The director met us at the front door, above which hung a sign that read:

> A NATION IS ALIVE
> WHEN ITS
> CULTURE IS ALIVE.

"Welcome," he smiled. "Please allow me to show you through as best I can. We have no electricity, but I have a flashlight."

Until 1992, this museum housed one of the finest collections of Asian art and artifacts in the world. Ten years later, there was little to see but rubble. We shivered in the musty chilled air as the director pointed his flashlight at piles upon piles of shattered ancient treasures. Most were either destroyed by the Taliban—who believed that any portrayal of a human form was sacrilege—or by bombs. Somehow, the director seemed optimistic about its recovery. "With international assistance, we are sure we can restore most of this," he said.

Our final visit of the day was to the Allahoddin Orphanage, home to hundreds of girls and boys on the outskirts of Kabul. Immediately upon entering the gray cement façade, we were surrounded by shouting crowds of children, from tiny toddlers to teenagers. Little hands pulled on my jacket and grasped to hold my hand, eager for human contact. Although initially unnerved by their sticky fingers and unwashed faces, I was soon reaching out and hugging everyone within my reach.

"We only have that one pump for water," announced the director, a middle-aged bespectacled man with a short gray-streaked beard. "And our plumbing rarely works," he added, pointing at the small water pump in the courtyard. "The children make a game out of pumping the water and filling buckets." Sure enough, the kids were jumping around the pump, energetically taking turns at keeping the water flowing into receptacles.

Inside the girls' quarters, I noticed a tiny child quietly sitting alone. Through the chill and dank air, her dark eyes stared with an expression beyond sadness and hope. One thin arm extended from the baggy sleeve of her oversized tan-and-yellow dress as she repeatedly crayoned the same simple pattern on a piece of paper.

The director gathered a group of children, aged four to fourteen, for us to photograph. A fifth-grade class of girls sang to us in Dari, the language of northern Afghanistan: "My mother is gone away. Afghanistan, you are now my mother, and I must take care of you."

Afterward, the director took us aside to explain the direness of the situation here. "When the Taliban took over Kabul in 1996, they came here and threw all the girls out in the street, taking some of the older ones with them. We don't know where they are now. Please help us in any way you can. Money would be best."

We distributed the pillows and wool mittens that we'd purchased in town for this purpose. These gifts seemed like a paltry contribution, but it was all we could do at the moment. As we drove off, I tried to envision life for women in this nation. In the 1990s, Afghanistan was modernizing and women lived fairly progressive lives.

The Taliban, of course, changed everything. Suddenly, these modern women were confined to their houses with all their windows painted black, permitted outside only when accompanied by a male relative. They were beaten for showing even a bit of wrist or ankle. They were denied an education or access to earning a livelihood and deprived of medical care. They were forbidden from visiting the public bath on occasion, even if they had no running water at home.

Somehow, the Afghan people's resiliency persisted, perhaps bolstered by their sense of humor. The Afghan women I befriended during this visit and subsequent trips mocked the Taliban-imposed restrictions. They cracked jokes about many things, including the blue burqas they had been forced to wear. One evening at an all-women's party, our hostess pretended to address a large crowd, asking: "Will the woman in the blue burqa please stand up?" Everyone giggled. Continuing the joke, another woman waved her arm as if signaling to an imaginary coat-check girl: "Mine's the blue one."

At first, I was surprised at these jokes, yet their laughter was infectious. Soon, we were doubled up in laughter, rolling amidst the cushions on the floor, trying to avoid the plates of kebabs and fruit.

Having worked with Afghan women who were living in exile in France and Tajikistan, I was accustomed to their hospitality, courage, and wit. But because of our stereotype of the Afghan man as a misogynist warrior, I did not know what to expect during my interactions with men. Yet, even in the dusty chaos of Kabul's perpetual traffic gridlock, I never saw any men get angry. My driver used the traffic jams to shout messages to other drivers and passengers. "Tell my cousin to ask his friend Hamid about the tire he is fixing for me." Even when cars crashed into each other, the drivers didn't seem very upset. Once, one of my drivers knocked a man off his bicycle. They chatted about it for a few minutes, then laughed and drove on.

On one of my last days in Kabul, Tarek, a university student, and I hiked up the side of a mountain near the city's ancient walls, which date from the fifth century. Some twenty-feet-high and twelve-feet-thick, these walls ascend almost perpendicularly from the Kabul River. As we clambered up the loose shale on the steep hillside, security helicopters buzzed above, while far below, women washed clothes in the trickle of river remaining after five years of drought.

On that day, most people were heading toward the Ghazi Sports Stadium. This was the infamous stadium where the Taliban performed public executions and stonings every Friday until they were routed by U.S. and Northern Alliance forces earlier in the year. Today's event was a commemoration in honor of Ahmad Shah Massoud, the great Afghan freedom fighter who was assassinated on September 9, 2001, two days before the attack on the Twin Towers in New York City. Al Qaeda is believed to have orchestrated the killing to deprive the United States of Afghanistan's most capable allied commander.

Up in the mountains, the hum of the city softened

and the air grew slightly less choked with dust. Most people in Kabul have a hacking cough or bronchitis, and I did too—a worrisome condition given that the air particles are believed to contain depleted uranium from Soviet and U.S. bombings. Children waved at us from doorways of mud-brick houses cantilevered into the slope so that one end of each roof was at ground level. A woman yelled something to Tarek. He translated: "She said that I should assist you more as the hillside is slippery."

At the next house up the slope, a one-legged man on crutches waved and shouted, too, beckoning us over with a smile. "He's inviting us to come in and have tea with him and his family," Tarek explained.

As we approached, I could see that he had the movie-star good looks of many Afghan men: gorgeous symmetrical features, muscular build, dark hair and beard, and expressive dark eyes. Afghan eyes really look into you, and their gaze is not pained or demanding or threatening in any way. It is dispassionate and composed, perhaps the result of millennia of survival.

"English? American?" the man asked. "Don't you have hills like this? Stay here awhile, and you'll get stronger legs. See what it's done for me!" He pointed to his stump and laughed. His four children peeked out from behind him as he ushered us into the living room. There was no electricity, but windows cut through the mud brick let in daylight. Unlit oil lamps sat in one corner.

Introducing himself as Ashraf, our host lowered himself onto a pillow on the dirt floor and indicated that we do the same. His wife, a beautiful woman with golden-green eyes, nodded hospitably as she brought in a teapot, cups, and bowls of nuts and raisins. With Tarek translating, we all settled in for a cozy visit.

"I'm the mayor of this section of the city," he said, a broad smile on his face. "I've fought against the Soviets and the Taliban to protect my family and little community here." A mine had blown off one of his legs, he explained, and he showed me various holes in his chest and back from mortar fire. He'd even been friends with Ahmad Shah Massoud, serving with him in both wars against the Soviet Union as well as the Afghan civil wars against the Taliban.

Yet, despite his personal tragedy, Ashraf was one of the most jovial people I've ever met, cracking jokes and grinning. As we talked, I realized that his knowledge of world affairs would put many Americans to shame. Where did he learn so much?

"I've never had time to go to school, but I listen to the BBC in Dari," he explained.

"My husband is a very good man," his wife chimed in.

Given the amount of affection he showed toward their children and to her, this seemed sincere. Still, I wanted to probe more deeply. What did he think of the cruel treatment his country had inflicted upon its women? Didn't he want his daughters to receive an education and find a good job?

He gave this some thought, then responded: "I'm an Islamist. I believe that women should have full rights to have careers, to go to university, but still, they should wear the hijab. We are Muslims; we want to respect our women wearing the cover. It is not the burqa that is the point but the freedom to move about in their lives, to live full lives, that is important."

"But it's uncomfortable inside the burqa and difficult to see and to walk," I persisted. "I tried one, and it gave me a headache. Do you think I'm a bad woman because I'm wearing trousers and a sweater with only a scarf around my neck? Look how nice it is for us to discuss life and everything together!"

He laughed and nodded in agreement.

We sipped tea with Ashraf for nearly two hours, sharing stories about our families, our travels, our lives as we pushed bowls of raisins back and forth. Finally, I said: "Here you are, after twenty-plus years of war. You've lost a leg, your body has been shot again and again, yet you are so cheerful. How is that?"

"Diane," he said, leaning forward from where he sat as he gestured toward me, "now we have peace," he said. "And peace is everything."

Postscript: I returned to Afghanistan several years later and life was going well there, but sadly, those few years of peace vanished again for these wonderful people and this war-torn country. I hope for a better future for my dear friends there.

Reading Group Discussion Questions

1. What are some differences you've experienced while traveling alone or with someone? What do you like and dislike about each mode of travel? Think about destinations or situations in which you would prefer traveling alone versus traveling with someone.

2. How are the experiences different for a woman and a man traveling? What are some examples from your life?

3. Sexual freedom: What does this mean? How might this be different for men and women?

4. Is it possible to lead an independent life while enjoying long-term love and companionship?

5. Have you had encounters with strangers in foreign lands that led you to new wisdom and understanding?

6. While traveling, have you encountered scary, possibly dangerous, experiences? If so, how did you deal with them, and how did it work out?

7. What effects and influences, good and bad, do we as Americans have on people of other cultures?

8. What can Americans learn from other cultures? What are some examples of how humor may differ among cultures?

9. What ingredients constitute "home" for you wherever you are?

10. How do the two epigrams at the beginning of the book, by Homer and Virginia Woolf, help focus on the themes and ideas of the book?

And now have I put in here, as thou seest, with ship and crew, while sailing over the wine-dark sea to men of strange speech.
— Homer, *The Odyssey*, 1.178

All women together ought to let flowers fall upon the tomb of Aphra Behn…for it was she who earned them the right to speak their minds. It is she—shady and amorous as she was—who makes it not quite fantastic for me to say to you to-night: Earn five hundred a year by your wits.
— Virginia Woolf

Publication Notes

Some of these stories have been previously published, in slightly different forms or with different titles.

"The Trout Baron" in *France: A Love Story: Women Write about the French Experience*, under the title "The Fisher Baron's Secret" (Seal Press 2004)

"An Italian Bedtime Story" in *The Best Women's Travel Writing*, Vol. 12 (Travelers' Tales 2020) and *Travel Stories from Around the Globe* (Bay Area Travel Writers 2012)

"Love on the Line" in *Salon Magazine* (June 1999, editor Don George)

"At Home in Afghanistan" in *The Best Women's Travel Writing 2010* (Travelers' Tales) under the title "Tea in Kabul"

"Saved by Colette: Seduction in St. Tropez" in *Erotic Travel Tales 2* (Cleis Press 2003) under the title "Heartburn"

"The Fertile Lands of Ancient Greece" in *Greece, A Love Story: Women Write about the Greek Experience* under the title "Dancing on the Wine-Dark Sea" (Seal Press 2007)

"In Colette's Boudoir: At Home in a French Château" in *B for Savvy Brides* (Spring 2000)

"At Home with the Water Buffalo Baronessa" in *Taste of Travel: Food Stories & Photos from Around the World* (Bay Area Travel Writers 2017)

Awards

2020

"Women in Morocco: Up Against the Wall," Silver Award, Solas Travelers' Tales

"An Unexpected New Year's Eve in Luxor," Bronze Award, Solas Travelers' Tales

"An Italian Bedtime Story: Chloroformed, Robbed, and Propositioned on an Italian Train," one of thirty-four out of thirteen-hundred selected to be in the anthology, *Best Women's Travel Writing Vol. 12*, Travelers' Tales Publications, 2020

2019

"Song of the Sirens," Silver Award, Solas Travelers' Tales

"Crumbs in an Egyptian Bedroom," "Cuba: Machismo and Feminism Together at Last," and "An Italian Bedtime Story," Solas Travelers' Tales Award Honorable Mentions

2017

"At Home in Afghanistan," Gold Award, Bay Area Travel Writers Annual Awards

"Dancing on the Wine-Dark Sea," Bronze Award, Solas Travelers' Tales—Women's Travel

2015

"Dinner in Dushanbe, Tajikistan," Bronze Award, Solas Travelers' Tales—Adventure Travel

2011

"My Dinner with Terrorists," Silver Award, Solas Travelers' Tales—Women's Travel

2010

"Tea in Kabul" ("At Home in Afghanistan"), Gold Award, Solas Travelers' Tales—Women's Travel

2007

"The Trout Baron," Gold Award, Solas Travelers' Tales—Love Story on the Road

Acknowledgments

It truly took an international village to support, encourage, and nudge me to complete this work. Much appreciation and thanks are due to so many. I can mention only a few of you dear folks:

To Linda Watanabe McFerrin, who edited, worked with me throughout the entire volume, and kept assuring me it was a beautiful book. To Matthew Felix for his continual words of wisdom, encouragement, and helping bring the book to market. To dear friends, Laurie McAndish King and Suzie Rodriguez for editorial advice, encouragement, and friendship. On my desk is a handmade pseudo-library card Suzie presented me on my birthday many years ago for a book that was entitled "She realized that she alone was the author of her biography: The Shocking Memoirs of a 20th Century Renegade." There are imagined reviews of my book from Simone de Beauvoir, Gloria Steinem, Anita Bryant, Chaucer, Dali, and F. Scott Fitzgerald. Suzie ends the card with the words: "Let's celebrate your publication next year at this time…!" Well, I'm a few years late but here it is!

Enormous gratitude for the art and skills of Jim Shubin for my gorgeous book cover, book design, and publication. To my many editors over the years, including Lavinia Spalding for her precise editing and encouragement, Camille Cusumano, Larry Habegger who published many of my essays in Travelers' Tales publications and gave them numerous awards, Don George (who published my first travel essay in *Salon* those many years ago) and to Adair Lara and her writing group. Special thanks to Tim Cahill, my longtime guru, who continues to lead the way with his wit, irony, and that "narrative arc in the sky." Much appreciation for the fastidious copy editing of Bob Cooper.

Of course, ongoing gratitude to my "writing village": my friends and colleagues in the Bay Area Travel Writers and Left Coast Writers for their love, enthusiastic support, and wise advice along the way, including Kimberly Lovato and Erin Bryne.

For their encouragement and love over many years: John Montgomery who experienced and photographed some of these adventures with me. To my stepdaughters, Kathleen Chance and Kimberly Montgomery for their wise and witty perspectives. To old friend Marv Mann who has been there for me over so many of my life's triumphs and challenges, especially during my feminist revolutionary years in academia and my horse show life.

To Jim Martin who helped my life shine more brightly every day.

To my seven-thousand college students over many decades and three countries for their enthusiasm, insights, and fun.

Of course, at the heart of it all, my gratitude to my mother Audrey who always reminded me to enjoy the dance of life. To my father Carlton, a great humanitarian who modeled how we all should care for others. To my amazing and talented brother Howard, an internationally renowned concert pianist and my earliest model of how to live a creative and intellectually curious life but who left us much too soon. And, finally, to my Aunt Bea who would have enjoyed all these stories.

About the Author

Diane LeBow grew up atop the Jersey Palisades on the Hudson River, close to Manhattan. After graduating from Douglass College (the women's college at Rutgers University), she earned an M.A. in English Literature at U.C. Berkeley. Next, after marrying a Dutch medical student, she lived for four years in the Netherlands, where she taught at the International School in The Hague, traveled extensively around Europe, and absorbed European lifestyle and values.

She then moved back to the States with her husband, first to New York City and then to the Bay Area in California. After a divorce, Diane taught for thirty-five years at Cañada College south of San Francisco. During that period, she returned to graduate studies, completing a Ph.D. at U.C. Santa Cruz in the History of Consciousness Department with a focus on feminist history and women writers.

Over the years, Diane has traveled to nearly one hundred countries. She has spent time with Afghan women, the Hopi, tribal people living on the Amazon, Tuvans, Mongolians, Corsicans, and Parisians. She has scuba-dived with sharks in the Red Sea, ridden a camel through locust swarms on the Libyan Sahara, and searched for the descendants of Amazon women who may live among Mongolian horsewomen.

Diane's writing has appeared in *Salon, Via, Image,* Cleis, Seal, Schocken, Travelers' Tales and many other publications. Her numerous awards include thirteen Solas Awards and a Lifetime Achievement Award from Douglass College (AADC, Rutgers University) for her writing, photojournalism, women's rights work, and as a pioneer of women's studies and innovative college teaching in Paris, Holland, and the USA. She has trained national champion Morgan horses, been a feminist organizer and AFT president, and is President Emerita of the Bay Area Travel Writers. The National Endowment for the Humanities and the Ford Foundation have awarded her grants. Diane lives in San Francisco when not on the road.

Diane's website is www.dianelebow.com.